The Triumph of Diversity

Rejoice in and Benefit from the Interconnectedness of Humankind

Arthur P. Ciaramicoli, Ed.D., Ph.D.

Published by Open Books

Copyright © 2020 by Arthur P. Ciaramicoli

Interior design by Siva Ram Maganti

ISBN-13: 978-1948598293

"Dr. Ciaramicoli takes diversity down a new path by focusing on its relationship with empathy and its ability to transform communities. Rather than thinking of diversity simply as an obligation to promote fairness among all of us, he demonstrates how diversity can act as a catalyst for increasing empathy and compassion within social networks. Dr. Ciaramicoli supports his theories through the latest research in the fields of diversity and empathy as well as intriguing stories from his private practice with individual patients and groups. By shedding light on the power of diversity and its direct relationship with empathy, he has made an important contribution to the field of mental health. I found this book riveting and hard to put down."

—Abbie Rosenberg, RN,
NP Psychotherapist and Founder/Executive Director Mental
Health Collaborative, Hopkinton, MA

"I laud this book as a critically important 'must read' by politicians, teachers, students, CEOs, clergy, neighbors and all whose hearts want to live in a better world. As a second-generation Holocaust survivor, I embody not only the pain of my parents, but also the first hand experiences of prejudice in this country of 'freedom and justice for all.' Much prejudice has to do with ignorance, passed on from generation to generation. Dr. Ciaramicoli has offered clearly how curiosity, education and interaction between diverse cultures, ethnicities, races, religions and belief systems can develop the empathy needed to embrace one another's differences for our individual benefit and that of all mankind."

—Eva Friedner,
M.A, M.S., Adult Child of Holocaust Survivors

"With his ecumenical approach to religions, Dr. Arthur Ciaramicoli comes across as a holy man pleading with his fellow American citizens who are getting sicker and meaner to change their dysfunctional ways and rediscover their mutilated humanity. Diversity, in the author's hand, is not a mere cliché but a genuine life saver. This book is an impressive primer on how to manage and, perhaps, even overcome deeply seated prejudices that are endangering our nation and the world."

—Dr. Anouar Majid, author of
Islam and America: Building a Future Without Prejudice, director
of the Center for Global Humanities and associate professor for
global initiatives at the University of New England

"Dr. Ciaramcoli's book, *The Triumph of Diversity* provides a much needed understanding of the spiraling rate of religious and cultural bias in our country today, and indeed, globally. It addresses in a compassionate and professional manner our psychic woundedness in our ourselves and in families that can give way to prejudice and distorted thinking about each other, as well as practical insight in how we can actually change our beliefs for the better. It is a must read in the times we live!"

—Fr. Carl Chudy,
Metrowest Interfaith Dialogue Project

"In the face of the daily acts of hatred and violence that confront us, Dr. Ciaramicoli offers an inspiring vision of human potential and an insightful prescription to achieve it. Read this heartfelt treatise on the human condition and be prepared for initial angst and ultimate upliftment."

—Siri Karm Singh Khalsa,
Minister of Sikh Dharma

"Dr. Ciaramicoli weaves clinical psychology and statistics into the fabric of lived experiences, offering the reader the triumphs that result from courage, empathy, equity, and unity."

—Dr. Carol Cavanaugh,
Superintendent of Schools, Hopkinton, Massachusetts

"I have read each of Dr. Ciaramicoli's books and this is by far his most important work, addressing the increase in hate crimes and the divisive climate that now exists in our country. Dr. Ciaramicoli not only describes the origin of hate crimes but he provides us with the means to lessen prejudice, hate and discrimination. I wish every adult in America would read this book, incorporate the wisdom it provides, and help return our country to a caring, compassionate land."

—**Dr. Robert Cherney, Chief Psychologist,
Advocates Community Health Services,
Framingham, Massachusetts**

"Although Dr. Ciaramicoli is a licensed psychologist he indeed is actually doing ministry and chaplaincy work. He is devoted to getting people to walk toward their fears of people who are different than themselves. He brings people together and encourages curiosity of other. He seeks to create unity by teaching about dialogue, empathy and compassion. He is on a crusade to help people love, not hate."

—**Dr. Rev. Frank Caruso,
Clinical Psychologist and Episcopal Minister**

"As a female surgeon with an ethnic background I certainly have encountered prejudice and discrimination. Dr. Ciaramicoli's chapter on the Me-Too Movement was poignant and powerful. As he says, it is critical to expand our empathy to understand and defeat dangerous stereotypes. Please take the time to read this book, it contains the wisdom we need to not only stop hate but it contains the wisdom to prevent hate."

—**Dr. Mary Bethony,
President of All About Women**

"I have been in a leadership position in the corporate world for over 30 years. The climate today is clearly less inclusive than in the past. Our political and corporate leaders need to have the integrity and empathy that Dr. Ciaramicoli describes as necessary to reduce discrimination while realizing that diversity is an asset not a disadvantage. Dr. Ciaramicoli has proven through credible research and his own personal and professional experiences that diversity is a tremendous advantage to our lives personally and professionally. Read this book and share it with as many people as you can, it is a path to a more just society and world."

—**Richard Werner, President and Chief Operating Officer,**
RC Werner and Associates, LLC

"As an Iranian Organizational leadership psychologist living in the United States, I believe Dr. Ciaramicoli's perspective in *The Triumph of Diversity* is exactly what we need in our modern world: Forgiveness. This book makes me think about forgiveness. To me, forgiveness is the art of acceptance and acknowledgment. We have to let go of what had happened in the past and embrace the future for the sake of our thriving society. Forgiveness will also help us build an active, compassionate, and empathic world. A world that, instead of addressing polaristic differences that will intrigue hate crimes, will encourage thoughtful leaders to celebrate diversity and establish a common ground for dialogue and human inspiration. Dr. Ciaramicoli's insights and wisdom are a must read for all of us who long for a more just, compassionate world."

—**Dr. Eissa Hashemi**

"Dr. Ciaramicoli's thoughts and research on diversity are broad and deep. Those of us in the field of education are accustomed to considering the importance of diversity, but thanks to this book, my perspective has been expanded and I am left with a sense of excitement and hope for our institutions, our communities and our purpose as educators."

—**Dr. Kevin Mahoney,**
Assistant Professor of Education, St. Joseph College, Maine

To Ariana and Carmela:
May your world be free of prejudice and blessed with the
fruits of Diversity

Contents

Introduction

"My Country is the World; My Religion is to do Good."

—Thomas Paine

I AM WRITING THIS book because I am broken hearted about recent developments in our society. I hope through the exploration of the topics I will share with you that we can address the rising tendencies of prejudice and hate within our culture, while discovering a formula to counter the fear of diversity and difference. I will tell you stories about people who have overcome prejudice and stereotypes, from neo-Nazi white supremacists to a teenage Muslim boy, from religious, business, and education leaders to ordinary everyday people. I will show you how having an open mind and an open heart has enriched their lives, and how it will enrich yours, too.

I have always believed that as Americans we are the leaders of the free world. Yet I am saddened by the number of Americans who don't seem to care about others in the world, or about those who seem different from us, or who seem to threaten our beliefs if theirs are dissimilar. I have been haunted by a comment made by one of my Latino clients: "If you are Jewish, brown, black or of any other than heterosexual orientation, you are no longer wanted in America." I hope with every fiber of my being that his perspective is not wholly accurate.

Most historians and social commentators agree that

America today is more polarized than at any time since the Civil War. Such polarization not only suggests individual and societal confusion, but begs answers to a number of questions: Have we as a society come to a time when differences in color, religion, sexuality or nationality are seen as threats to our way of life? Has exclusion and lack of interest in those suffering in other parts of the world become a knee-jerk response meant to somehow protect us from our own irrational fears?

Groupthink is a concept developed by psychologist Irving Janis in 1971. Janis defined groupthink as the psychological drive for consensus at all costs, which suppresses disagreement and prevents the appraisal of alternatives in cohesive decision-making groups.

When we close the door on those who seem dissimilar, we limit our own potential for growth, and ultimately, our happiness. Diversity is the antidote to groupthink. It expands the mind and enriches the soul.

Disdain of diversity almost always manifests as an us/them dichotomy, an in-group and an out-group, which is often the dynamic elemental to the creation of cults and the normalization of dogmatic thinking. The out-group is disdained, if not totally condemned. A stereotypical view of the out-group is maintained, with direct pressure on dissenters to conform to narrow perspective. Groupthink often creates an illusion of invulnerability and unanimity.

Such groups attract the insecure and the fragile among us, offering a convoluted certainty to lives that have been lived with ambivalence and uncertainty.

But the opposite is true of diverse groups, those which share ideas from many different perspectives absent of the threat of not conforming. Ideas flow and minds expand as a result of variety and novelty.

In contrast to the growth in ethnocentrism, a movement is taking place throughout the world called

deliberate polling (a random, representative sample of people engaged in deliberation on current issues through small group discussions, with experts as moderators, for the purpose of creating more understanding and broadening thoughtful reflective opinion). This movement brings individuals of varying perspectives, including those from opposite points of view on various subjects, to a civil dialogue on many issues. The result seems to be that fixed views can change when people have a chance to hear opposing views and examine facts without bias or outside influence. According to Professor James Fishkin of Stanford University, the creator of this process, about 70% of participants change their minds.

America in One Room

Recently a project called America in One Room, an example of deliberate polling, gathered 526 people from 47 states in Grapevine, Texas for a weekend of bi-partisan discussions regarding the major political issues of our time. Pre-discussion and post-discussion surveys were conducted. Interestingly people who felt that American democracy is working increased from 30% in the beginning of the event to 60% after the event. Participating individuals also said they felt less skeptical of those with opposing political views at the conclusion. Participants who thought that those on the opposite political side were not thinking rationally dropped from 51% to 33%. Most amazing was that 95% stated that by participating they learned a great deal from those they had previously considered to be very different from them. Group discussions, when facilitated by experienced leaders, can lead not only to greater understanding, but to less conflict while increasing the chance of reaching compromise.

How Beliefs Change

This recent consultation is an example of the type of bias that can be altered with an empathic approach.

Luke is a midwestern Protestant who called for help with his anxiety in the workplace. Interestingly, he looks similar to country singer Luke Bryant; he is tall and lanky and speaks in a manner that conveys naiveté. His HR representative describes him as having difficulty with colleagues who are not like him. He becomes defensive with those who are not American born, and also those who do not support his rigid religious beliefs. He is seen as a talented contributor but uneasy with his Indian colleagues as he often retreats in their presence. During our first meeting he mentioned that he was glad I was a Christian so he could feel free to talk openly. "My last psychologist was Jewish, and I just couldn't relate to him." I asked Luke why and he could not specify: "It was just a feeling, an uneasiness."

When the origin of prejudice cannot be identified it is often the result of conditioning from the past that was not examined earlier in an objective manner. What we hear in our homes can easily become a belief in a young person's mind.

I inquired if Luke had had experience with Jewish colleagues or Jewish friends. "We didn't have any Jews in our town; no blacks, no Asians, just people like me." I asked him why he assumed I was Christian. "Because of your last name. Aren't you Italian?" I answered in the affirmative but also let him know that there are Italian Jews in Italy, and in this country, too. One thousand or more Italian Jews died in Auschwitz, and it is estimated that 45,000 Jews live in Italy currently. Suddenly Luke looked uneasy. His comfort level had dissipated based on a new classification of the person in front of him.

In my experience, Luke's story is fairly typical. He

believed what he'd learned early in life from authority figures—parents, teachers and clergy—lessons based on distortions that were passed down from generation to generation. But as we formed a bond Luke gradually became open to examining each of the ideas embedded in his psyche that may or may not have been true. His fear of my being Jewish dissipated through the empathic bond we formed. He gradually felt more open to question me and to explore his own belief system. For instance, he asked why Jews would not accept that Jesus was the Messiah. My answer: "How could they when the Messiah, according to Jewish scripture, is expected to create an age of universal peace, end all hatred, oppression and suffering, and unite humanity through the knowledge of the God of Israel, none of which he did." To his credit, Luke listened and learned. "Jews are not disparaging Jesus, they simply are adhering to the signs that they believe would indicate the Messiah's presence. Slowly, Luke's empathic range expanded. Over time he became comfortable within the diverse world in which he lives.

It is a scientific fact that when we form empathic bonds, we change brain chemistry for the better, producing the near miracle neurotransmitter oxytocin, which creates trust and a willingness to listen and to learn.

After 18 months of weekly meetings, Luke began a session by asking why he had never seen my wife or kids in the yard or around the house (I work from an office in my home). I responded, "What makes you think I have a wife and kids?" With a mischievous grin on his face he said, "Oh, great; now you're going to tell me you're an Italian, *gay* Jew." I asked Luke if it would matter. "Not any more, Doc," he said, "we're past all that foolishness." Mission accomplished.

The Triumph of Diversity

The experience I had with Luke over those months is similar to the experience I have had with many individuals, particularly those who have joined my leadership and communication groups. Those groups, which have been ongoing for more than 30 years, are populated by Iranian Christians, Indian Hindus, British Episcopalians, Australian Protestants, black central Africans, gay men, lesbian women, obese individuals and straight white Americans. The members of the group appear to be different on the outside, but over time each comes to understand their shared humanity. **Such an experience is infectious; once a person learns how to relate empathically to others, he feels more comfortable and more secure in the world.** A brain change has taken place that markedly reduces fear and the need to be afraid of differences; empathy opens the door to commonalities.

Hopefully, this process can be manifested in all of our lives so that we may counter the divisiveness currently gaining momentum within our country. We are in desperate need of more of those who unite rather than ostracize.

Now, let's examine the recent resurgence of hate and prejudice within our culture.

Anti-Semitic occurrences reached a record high in 2018. The Anti-Defamation League recorded 1,879 incidents of vandalism, harassment or attacks. The worst attack at a Pittsburgh synagogue left 11 people dead, the most dreadful attack in modern history in the United States. The greatest amount of hate crimes against any religious group targeted Jews, an increase of 664 from 2015 to 2016.

The number of assaults against Muslims rose significantly from 2015 to 2016. There were 307 incidents of anti-Muslim hate crimes in 2016, a 19% increase in one year. The total number of anti-Muslim incidents rose 67% from 2014 to 2015.

Regardless of political persuasion, we must work to end Islamophobia and anti-Semitism because the struggle is the same: to preserve diversity, inclusiveness and the freedom to be and speak without fear of reprisal.

Half of all hate crimes in the United States are race related (the FBI indicates that 47% of hate crimes are racially motivated). Two thousand thirteen incidents involving black or African American as victims occurred in 2017. The majority of Americans believe race relations have worsened.

LBGTQ workers also face considerable discrimination in the workplace. One out of every 25 complaints about discrimination is reported by LGBTQ employees. Transgender workers experience even higher discrimination, with 97% experiencing harassment. Additional studies have found a significant negative bias toward LBGTQ individuals in the medical community as well, making it harder to obtain quality medical care.

In a Pew research center survey in 2017, 42% of women said that they had experienced some form of gender discrimination. One in five women said they had been sexually harassed at work, while one in five women under age 30 said they had been sexually harassed online.

Three years ago, the United States ranked 28th in gender equality according to the World Economic Forum study of 149 countries. Last year, the US ranked 51st.

An analysis of 214 studies and 91,000 teenagers in the *Journal The American Psychologist* found that perceived discrimination led to depression, low self-esteem, lower academic performance, lower motivation, substance abuse and risky sexual behavior. Other reports have found that women who reported sex discrimination were three times more likely to experience clinical depression.

However, many under the age of 40 still want and seek out diversity. They are the most diverse group of Americans in our history. They have rejected old stereotypes, racial divisions and prefer to work with and live in communities composed of various ethnic groups. They are as we all should be, committed to not allowing our communities to be divided along religious or racial lines. The most successful American cities, like Boston, Seattle, Chicago, and Washington have significant numbers of ethnic groups and all have thriving LGBTQ communities. A study in *Psychology, Public Policy, and Law* found that US cities with greater gender pay equality had more advanced laws against sexual orientation-based discrimination.

The encouraging news, according to a 2019 CNN and Kaiser Family Foundation poll, is that 81% of Americans say that the increasing number of people from different ethnic groups, different races and different nationalities is enriching American culture. This is an increase from 70% in 2016. There is, however, an increase in those who believe ethnic and racial discrimination has worsened. The survey also indicated that Latino Americans and blacks report that they feel their lives are in more danger than they were in 2015.

The Empathy Dilemma

Empathy is the capacity to understand and respond to the unique experiences of another. It is essentially the ability to see beyond the surface and into the heart and soul of another. Countries with higher levels of empathy, according to a Michigan State University study, have higher levels of self-esteem, agreeableness, conscientiousness, well — being, prosocial behavior and collectivism. Unfortunately, in recent years there has been a reduction in empathy and an increase in self-absorption in America. A study from the University of Michigan Institute for Social Research discovered that college students currently have higher levels of narcissism and lower levels of empathy than those of the previous generation.

Interestingly, additional studies found that women in their fifties are more empathic than any other group, with middle age adults being more empathic than older and younger adults. I imagine being immersed in motherhood has expanded empathy for many women, as well as women who have been caregivers, spouses or parents. Researchers have proven, however, that empathy can always be expanded, and that such expansion contributes to a sense of well-being. Hannah Schreier of Penn State University split Canadian high school sophomores into two groups. One group volunteered at a local elementary school, the other group was on a waiting list for volunteering. Three months later those who had volunteered had lower body index and significantly lower cholesterol levels. The most interesting result was that those who had the highest empathy had the lowest inflammation levels, and those with the highest altruism had the lowest cholesterol levels. Of course, this particular study was conducted with high school sophomores, so it is not clear what we might generalize about the adult population. Yet other studies have shown that volunteers who think about others decrease their mortality risk markedly. Empathic immersion in the lives of others changes our entire physiology for the better. One key way to increase empathy is to feel compassion for those suffering in the world, in your area, nationally and internationally. In other words, following Thomas Paine's quote, my favorite of all quotes. An exclusive approach to the world restricts empathy; ignoring oppression, wherever it takes place, robs us of our humanity.

I invite you to take the Prejudice Questionnaire when you complete the book.

1.

The Early Imprints:
Prejudicial Origins

"Prejudice is a learned trait. You're not born preju-
diced; you're taught it."

—Charles R. Swindoll

BY THE TIME I reached high school I had heard that
the Irish were drunks, the Italians were mobsters, the
Polish were dumb, blacks were lazy, Jews were cheap,
homosexuals were going to hell, atheists were evil, and
the Chinese and Russians were inherently bad people.

I'm not exactly sure how I realized in my adolescence
that these comments were all inaccurate and prejudicial, but from an early age I was sensitive to these and
other distortions. My guidance counselor told me in
my senior year of high school that I was not college
material; he said I would just flunk out and disgrace
my family and my school. I obtained one of the highest scores on an IQ test and my guidance counselor
accused me of cheating; he could not imagine that I
could excel on my own ability.

I did a postgraduate year of high school at Bridgton
Academy in Maine, a school noted for helping athletes
who did not perform well academically in high school

to learn how to study. When I graduated the caption above my name in the Bridgton yearbook read, *"BA's Number One WAP, Tough as Nails."* In fact, I am not *"tough as nails"* but learned early in life not to seem fearful when confronted by bullies. When I was eight years old I was walking home with my cousin Pasquale, who is five years older than I, when two older boys started taunting us. My cousin immediately looked me in the eye and said, *"Don't act scared; make them think you are fearless. Bullies always retreat."* I thought that was a crazy idea but out of fear I followed the instructions as we approached them, looked them in the eye with fury and just as my cousin had said, they backed down—a technique that I evidently fooled my Bridgton classmates with as well. I was called a WAP or Guinea many times subsequently, particularly during my college days, but I did not suffer to the degree that my black and Jewish friends did. Nevertheless, I did experience the emotions that accompany prejudice. Probably for that reason, or perhaps being close to a mother who felt deeply for those who were abused, I read everything I could find about the Holocaust and the enslavement of African Americans, and because of early lessons, both personal and abstract, I will always be deeply affected by the mindset that believes that it is permissible to enslave or kill others based on religion or the color of one's skin.

Parents Beware

Distorted views of others begin early in life, with parents having the greatest impact on the attitudes that their children eventually accept as truths.

Studies by Dr. Sonia Kang, a psychologist at the University of Toronto, found that between ages three and six children begin to stereotype and generalize based on what they hear from their parents. By fifth grade, however, children are more likely to base their opinions on their own experiences. The imprint of the early years is set however, and difficult to change without open environments that foster the appreciation of diversity rather than those that insist on adherence to group norms, regardless of how inaccurate their beliefs may be.

Conformity: Going along with Prejudice

Several studies have proven that discriminatory behavior is rooted in the desire to conform to the norms of the groups to which we belong. Apartheid created racial discrimination and prejudice for 46 years until the norms in South Africa changed. Those individuals who are likely to be conformist are also more likely to be more prejudiced. Similarly, it has been more acceptable to be prejudiced against black people in the southern United States than in the north where it has not been as tolerated.

One of my clients was a star football player in Idaho; there were no blacks on his state championship team, although he recalls that they played basketball and baseball. He grew up in a town where it was common for black kids to keep to themselves, sit with each other in the cafeteria and seldom sit at 'white' tables. To Brett, it seemed normal at his high school and in his community. Kids seem to be divided according to race, not formally, but everyone knew what was expected. Brett readily admits that when he earned a scholarship to play for a division one New England college team with black players, he felt uneasy. His parents had made disparaging remarks about blacks, Jews, Italians and Hispanics. He said he didn't really think about those groups much as a kid because neither he nor his family had any contact with any of those groups of people. Studies from Rush University and Yale University have demonstrated that children carry prejudices learned in childhood into adulthood, and those stereotypes then affect how they, as adults, interact with people of different backgrounds.

"It took me four years to unlearn everything I had heard about black people while growing up. So many un-truths and so much self-consciousness on my part! My beliefs were formed without any examination of the sources I was exposed to and looked up to. By the time I graduated I had black and Jewish friends, and I am now married to an Italian woman. No one at home would believe that!"

Brett's views changed over time because he was placed in close proximity to those he had only heard about but never had had personal experience.

Studies by Brandeis University psychologist Leslie Zebrowitz demonstrate that prejudice originates in part from negative reactions to unfamiliar faces. When subjects were exposed to faces they had seldom seen they increased their liking of these faces as exposure increased. The same is true with interactions. **Nothing reduces prejudice and racism more than having the courage to forge friendships with those considered different than yourself.** Remember, both sides fear rejection; so try to get past the fear as it is often based on inaccurate assumptions.

Certain media outlets would, for instance, have you believe that Muslim-Jewish relations are poor when in fact the truth is the opposite. The American Muslim Poll 2019: Predicting and Preventing Islamophobia found that Muslim-Jewish relations are currently excellent in the United States. Relations between the two groups have also been a chief focus of the American Jewish Committee Global Forum. Both groups hold the other in high regard, with only 10% of each side having negative attitudes toward the other. A recent Gallup poll found that those who report hatred toward Jews are 32 times as likely to feel the same toward Muslims. It is true that Jews are exposed to hate crimes the most, with hate crimes rising toward Muslims 67% in the last three years.

2.

The Fuel for Prejudice:
Distorted Beliefs

"The most fundamental aggression to ourselves, the most fundamental harm we can do to ourselves, is to remain ignorant by our not having the courage and respect to look at ourselves honestly and gently."

—Pema Chodron

I AWOKE THIS MORNING at 6:00 am, as I always do during the week. I got ready for my spinning class, had a great workout and felt exhilarated, looking forward to seeing my clients and group sessions this evening. I began perusing the news when I saw an awful picture of a beaten mother, Beronica Ruiz, and her 12-year-old son who were attacked while she held her one-year-old baby on a street next to her son's school in Passaic, New Jersey. The incident began when a 13-year-old boy chanted, "Go back to Mexico!" in the school cafeteria. Other boys joined with anti-immigrant slanders. Beronica's son, an American citizen, was told he would be beaten after school. School officials informed Mrs. Ruiz about the threats to her son so she came to the school to escort her son home. Three boys followed them, one punched her 12-year-old son, knocking him to the ground. Beronica stood between them, and a young boy punched her in the face. She lost consciousness as she fell to the sidewalk. Beronica had a concussion and facial fractures.

Beronica has subsequently received many calls from other parents saying their children have also been bullied.

The obvious question is, how does a 13-year-old boy develop such anger and hatred toward a fellow classmate? The answer surely is that somewhere along the line this young boy was taught to hate, and to justify cruel behavior. Obviously, if one grows up in a home hearing racial or ethnic slurs, that person will likely assume that his or her parents know the truth. That is how the conditioning begins. Prejudice is taught and reinforced by continued negative references to the unfortunate chosen group. When this type of prejudice turns into an actual brutal act there is usually subtle or overt permission granted by authority figures to develop and act upon sadistic tendencies. Cruelty is condoned and encouraged.

Sadistic-Narcissistic Parents

Parents with sadistic-narcissistic characters need to be in control, and they will humiliate children, usually picking on the most sensitive and vulnerable. Such parents will inflict emotional and physical pain, humiliating the weakest child and praising the seemingly tough child who is likely mimicking the behavior he or she sees. This type of parent displays a tremendous lack of empathy, and often does not have the love and desire to nurture that a healthy parent expresses with ease.

The following paragraph is an excerpt from an interview by Samantha Rodman with psychologist Dr. Sam

Vakim, a self-proclaimed narcissist.

"What parts of your upbringing may have contributed to your narcissism in later life?

"First being put on a pedestal, then idolized and forced to fulfill my mother's unrealized fantasies of grandeur, and then physically and psychologically tortured over a period of 13 years. Pathological narcissism is a reaction to prolonged abuse and trauma in early childhood or early adolescence. The source of the abuse or trauma is immaterial—the perpetrators could be parents, teachers, other adults, or peers.

"Pampering, smothering, spoiling, and 'engulfing' the child are also forms of abuse (and to a lesser extent lead to preoccupied attachment). I have had to endure both forms of maltreatment. Pathological narcissism is a defense mechanism intended to deflect trauma. The victim's 'True Self' turns into a 'False Self" which is omnipotent, invulnerable, and omniscient. The narcissist uses the False Self to regulate his or her sense of self-worth by obtaining narcissistic supply (any form of attention, both positive and negative."

The circumstances described by Dr. Vakim are not unfamiliar to anyone who has had a narcissistic parent or parents. These awful childhood experiences lead to a chronic fear of rejection, right into adulthood, making it difficult for the adult to trust another human being or allow another human being to know them on a deep level. Dr. Vakim, like many others, was blamed for behaviors that were innocent and should not have been punished by any reasonable parent. But rejection by a parent actually stimulates the same part of the brain that physical pain stimulates. This chronic pain can become unbearable and eventually lead to difficulties with alcoholism or other addictions, as the drug temporarily masks the pain and fear.

To Follow or Lead

Billy grew up in a small Alabama town with two alcoholic parents, both who were racist, anti-Semites and resentful of any person who was not of their Baptist faith. Their slurs were frequent and they left few people out of their sadistic orbit. Billy remembers his father's comments about a young gay boy who was beaten by several high school students. The story made front page news in the local paper, and as his dad drank his first Budweiser for breakfast he showed Billy the article and said, "If you ever become a fag, don't bother coming home." Both parents began the day with beer and cigarettes, critiquing the news and making derogatory comments on whatever was on the TV screen, including their tremendous distaste for overweight people.

Although Billy felt uncomfortable with his parents' anger, he did follow their coping style by drinking excessively in high school. He was given his first beer at age 13 by his father, and from that point onward drinking seemed to be a normal way of dealing with life. Billy's older sister was his saving grace. Beth loved to read; her way of escaping was through novels. She would pass books on to Billy, and as a result, her love of a great story became his as well. Remarkably, he earned a scholarship to a local college to play baseball, as sports also became his way to avoid the negativity and anger in his home. During the four years he excelled on his high school team, his parents never attended one game. Their absence fueled his sense of rejection, but his coaches saw his athletic potential. Their encouragement went beyond the athletic field as they tried to validate his keen mind. Billy's stature, at six feet five inches, helped him athletically, and his natural strength allowed him to throw a baseball at incredible speed. In college, Billy had gained a bit of self-confidence, but his internal anger and alcohol abuse continued to plague him. At times, particularly when drunk, he was prone to acting similarly to his parents. He was overly sensitive and overly reactive to humor directed his way. He was known to have started several fights when alcohol limited his judgment.

Billy is an example of how being humiliated early in life leads to intolerable shame, which often is expressed in anger and possibly rage. Despite his inner torment, he felt enormous guilt when he hurt people. In his early twenties, he moved to the Boston area for a sales position in the pharmaceutical industry. He met his wife Rachel at work, and she became a positive influence on his life. At one point Rachel insisted that Billy seek treatment for alcoholism, and that is how we met.

The Power of Group

I met with Billy for several sessions and then added him to one of my group sessions focused on improving interpersonal and communication skills. I often wonder how some people from horrible histories find it within themselves to change direction to become the person that has lain hidden within them all their lives. In Billy's case, the influence of his sister, his coaches and then Rachel led him to my door.

Initially, he found feedback from group members difficult, but as his ability to see beyond the surface improved, he could tell that they cared about him and were trying to help him free himself from addiction and a negative self-image. They coaxed out his potential, and the goodness that had lain dormant for so many years. When he ended his sessions two years later, he had become one of the most empathic members of the group, his insights were highly valued and his ability to be tactfully direct was impressive.

Billy has become a leader; he no longer follows the distorted perspectives of his parents. He is sober today, married with one son. He is a committed father and is immensely grateful for the journey he underwent to become a clear-thinking, compassionate, non-prejudicial human being.

Billy's experience tells us that we don't necessarily need a village to transform us, but we do need a few people who care deeply about us and who can serve as examples for empathy, compassion and an expanded view of the world.

3.

The Undoing of Prejudice:
Regaining the Truth

"Hate is on the rise in America; it's emboldened, normalized, and destroying lives. I've dedicated my life to pulling people out of hate, I know how these people think and how to help because I used to be one of them."

—Christian Picciolini

BILLY'S EXPERIENCE IN THE previous chapter is similar to the experience of other members of my leadership and communication groups. They come from different walks of life, women and men, all races, several ethnic groups and as well as several religious groups as well as atheists. Initially, they seem a bit uncomfortable with people that they have seldom encountered, but over time, as empathy expands, individuals begin to find common ground—the human ground. The old saying that we are more alike than we are different applies once people have had a chance to experience new ways of relating. Members learn from each other; they come to realize that diversity leads to expansion of one's mind, intellectual and emotional growth.

All the individuals in my groups are quite capable,

yet they have suffered emotionally due to negative and inaccurate views of themselves. Many have been the object of parental bias as well as taking in the biased views of others. Children who listen to bigotry and cruel comments about others often take on their parents' views without realizing that these inaccurate views are not based on facts. On whole, children can't identify with cruelty or feel comfortable with sadism (the enjoyment of hurting others). I have spent many years trying to identify the qualities in young people that prevent them from adopting distorted views. One consistent finding is the uneasiness a child feels when he senses a parent's desire to hurt others intentionally. One of my clients recently told our group that she idealized her father until the age of six or seven. "I could see the delight in his eyes when he talked about blacks, gays, fat people and Jews. The more he spewed his cruelty, the more I wanted to get away from him. Eventually, I knew I hated him as much as he hated those he targeted; at least I hated the joy he felt in disparaging people. And it wasn't just those groups he hated; he directed his hate to my sisters and to me as well. We were all beaten at different times, while my mother stood by silently and did nothing. *She had a Ph.D. in conflict avoidance.*"

Today, Carrie is a woman that all group members admire and view in highest regard. Her stories of growing up in the south, being told to stay away from black boys and doing the opposite displays a great degree of compassion for those who at first glance seem different. "I was the only white girl at our dances that would dance with the black boys. I wanted to make them feel comfortable and I wanted to get to know them. At first I felt uncomfortable. I had never talked to a black person, never mind dancing with a black boy. I noticed immediately that they were far more respectful than white boys. Little by little I learned through experience that my father was wrong—all his crazy ideas were wrong!"

Neo-Nazi Skinhead Becomes Leading Force Against Hate

As soon as I heard about Christian Picciolini's MSNBC "Breaking Hate" series, I started reading about his journey from being recruited into the neo-Nazi movement as a 14-year-old eighth grader to becoming one of America's leading forces in the anti-hate movement. I wanted to understand how a human being can change hatred into a fervent desire to help hate mongers change their views and learn the truth about those they have been told are less than human.

Christian has successfully launched the Free Radicals Project, a national movement to reduce hate and increase empathy toward others. He emphasizes the value of diversity and the richness of understanding and connection with those who seem different on the surface. Christian's project, his books and multiple interviews, are available online, so I am not going to describe his work in detail. My main reason for wanting to speak with Christian was to understand the process by which he gave up hate for love. I am grateful that Christian agreed to talk with me as he provided insight into how a prejudiced individual comes to perceive more accurately, and more truthfully.

Christian told me how he had felt abandoned as a child (he was also bullied and had a limited relationship with his passive father, who worked most of the time and didn't become involved with his son). He was recruited by the first neo-Nazi white nationalist in 1996. His fragile sense of self was immediately given a sense of pride, identifying him with a movement that would provide him with the family connections he longed for but had not experienced. This need to belong became almost addictive and was the force which led him to adopt extremist views.

Given this history, I asked Christian what happened that began his questioning of the conditioning he had so emphatically received. He told me that he'd started a music store in Chicago selling neo-Nazi music and white power music. He also traveled through Europe with a new-Nazi band promoting white nationalism music. His store became known for spreading neo-Nazi propaganda. Eventually, Jewish, black and gay individuals came into the store to challenge Christian's views.

His racist and anti-Semitic views began to gradually change as he encountered people that he found to be quite different than he had been told. He actually realized that these individuals were likeable and interesting. He eventually closed the store and began working for IBM at an entry-level job installing computers. He was sent to work at his former high school where he had caused much difficulty for teachers and administrators. He told me that he was anxious to return there as he expected criticism for the strife he had caused.

At this job he met a black security guard named Johnny Holmes. Christian described the interactions with Mr. Holmes as an important experience that further changed his view of black people. He realized through his increased familiarity with those he had been taught to hate that he had to unlearn the mythical ideas he had embraced. He describes the compassion he has received from those whom he hated and abused as a major reason for opening his eyes and heart to the world.

When we encounter those who are prejudiced against us with compassion, as in Christian's experience, we bring down walls. When we respond with aggression or fear we create a greater divide.

While Christian and I talked I was impressed with

his courage and openness, as I know he receives death threats daily but has refused to back down as he is extremely committed to telling the truth about hate groups. In fact, he has helped many young people leave hate groups and return to the society they had been taught to condemn.

The process that Christian describes is similar to what I have observed taking place in my leadership and communication groups. We develop prejudices based on ignorance of those we demonize, or those with whom we are simply not familiar. Once we have exposure to those whom we have never encountered, we are affected by actual experience rather than adopting dogma without actual, one-to-one experience. In the interview I conducted with Christian, I could also hear how he has expanded his range of empathy to understand and care for all people. His commitment to defeating hate is inspiring as well as his ability to acknowledge and take responsibility for the mistakes he has made and the people he has hurt.

Rising Above Prejudice

We all grow up with certain ideas about ourselves and the world and all the different kinds of people who occupy our planet. I believe our responsibility as adults is to find out the accuracy of what we learned. Are our ideas about ourselves accurate? Are ideas about those who we have not personally encountered accurate? Today, we live within an international climate. Classrooms are far more diverse than in years past. Business leaders travel to India, Japan, China, Thailand as well as forging partnerships in many other countries.

From an early age I heard my father make comments that I did not like. Later in life I helped him see how prejudicial some of his views were, and he seemed to become more open-minded, although I am not sure he believed that he was ever misguided. My mother had a softer heart and seldom made prejudicial statements, and I knew she had deep feelings for anyone who was suffering. So, like Carrie, why did I not adopt my father's views? My dad was a good man, a morale man and a hero in World War Two. Nevertheless, when his temper erupted, the generalizations he would utter were extreme. His anger, similar to Carrie's experience, made me feel distant from him. I could feel great uneasiness in my body when he would erupt and categorize others unfairly.

My mother seldom condemned others for prejudicial reasons. I have one memory that is encoded deep in my mind. My brother had taken his own life with an intentional heroin overdose at the age of 23. He was in Amsterdam and was sold very potent heroin by a Chinese man. At the time there were many articles in the *New York Times* and other newspapers about the increased potency of the heroin coming from China.

During a tender moment shortly after his death, my mother and I talked about his use of heroin. She made a generalization about the Chinese and I commented that this was one man's action and not necessarily representative of an entire culture. She became angry with me, somewhat atypical for her, and admonished me, "You are defending the chink that killed your brother!" I was shocked that she used that language but knew that she was devastated and couldn't control her anger, so the stereotype had escaped her lips. Yet, it was another learning moment for me. Here was a woman who was usually open minded, but under duress she had lashed out at an entire culture. When we are wounded, or when are broken hearted, it is hard to see clearly, and as a result generalizations seem to answer unanswerable questions and fill fathomless chasms. We need the eyes of others who are not so affected to gain proper perspective. My mother never mentioned the Chinese again; I am not sure whether she changed her mind or simply remained silent. I would like to believe the former.

The Physical Cost of Prejudice

We know that children who grow up in stressful homes have excessive amounts of the stress hormone cortisol in their systems. As a result, the telomeres in their bodies, the ends of each chromosome, shorten prematurely as a result, which ages these children years ahead of their biological age.

We also know that prejudice causes tension, and that the stress of the fear of others causes the release of the stress hormone cortisol. Cortisol causes several negative physical reactions such as inflammation, memory loss, anxiety, depression and weight gain.

Prejudice and discrimination sacrifices the truth, and whenever we live according to false beliefs about others, or about ourselves, we suffer.

Perceiving the truth is not just about seeing others accurately, it is also necessary to come to see oneself accurately. This only happens by re-examining the conclusions we came to early in life. We cannot accomplish this work alone; we are all too subjective, thus the need for feedback from others that we judge as accurate in their reading of other people.

Prejudice Goes Both Ways

I recently added a black man from Central Africa to one of my leadership and communication groups. He made a comment early in his first meeting that the white people in the group couldn't understand him or the suffering that those with his skin color suffer in this country. "I don't look like you, I don't sound like you and therefore I am a person white people want to stay away from."

After six months of attending the group, he began to see that he was generalizing, and that in fact he had been welcomed with warmth and an appreciation for his struggles. He told us that his name, Imani, means faith, and he realized that he had lost his faith in mankind as a result of a few comments made by a few prejudiced Americans.

The group accepted Imani, but to his surprise, some of his own prejudices emerged as he interacted with others. His description of his wife's behavior offended the women in the group. His blaming nature held her responsible for their daughter's struggles, as he saw parenting as primarily her role despite the fact that she worked full time as a nurse. On one occasion, one of the female members was talking about her husband's lung cancer and Imani responded by telling her, "You need to be positive, stop focusing on the worry, be strong and focus on other things." He then changed the subject by interjecting humor into the conversation. Paula was infuriated by his simplistic explanation and his tendency to want people to stay positive, and to stay away from anything too deep. Imani told us early on that he does not speak to his two sisters; he seldom spent time with his father, whom he described as punitive and mean to him and to his sisters, and especially toward his mother. He had become conflict-avoidant as a result, but had little awareness as to how he was continuing his father's view of women and parenting.

Imani's tendency to flee was seen by him as the only way to deal with a wife who was unappreciative. He viewed his daughter as spoiled, yet he had little to do with disciplining her other than coming home and yelling at her when she would not go to bed on time, or not get him tea when he ordered her to do so while he was on his iPad and lying upon the couch.

Imani has received truthful feedback based on careful empathic listening. He has been defensive when his image has been tarnished. Unfortunately, he did not display a desire to be open. He resorted to old defenses by trying to stop difficult emotional conversations with simplistic responses. He used what I call the 'grow up and get over it' theory of conflict resolution. Eventually, he started missing meetings and ultimately did not return.

Don't we all Have Biases

Some members of Imani's group were surprised when they learned of his biased views of women, while others were not. Some group members assumed that because he had suffered prejudice himself he would have been an open-minded person. Others expected his views would be rigid from the way he blamed his wife for their arguments, while he excused his own tendency toward anger and to quickly escalate conflict. Many of the women in the group clearly felt bad for him. None of the men seemed to relate to him, seeing him as more of a victim and a caster of blame.

In this particular case, the women who viewed Imani in a positive way seemed to minimize Imani's negative qualities (interestingly, they had the same dynamic in their tension-filled marriages). They reacted with sympathy, a quick reaction of compassion without knowing the complete story. The men, for the most part, did not minimize his flaws; they, in turn, seemed more impatient with his tendency to blame. Imani was a victim of prejudice, but not a victim in his marriage or his extended family.

Rita, a 46-year-old divorced woman who had been

in the group for some time, was the only female who had not trusted Imani from the outset. She was quite adept at reading people, especially those who chronically blame. She had suffered in several relationships by feeling sorry for men who did not display the ability to reciprocate. She had been fooled one too many times by allowing herself to be manipulated by a sad story.

Imani helped group members learn that just because a person has been discriminated against doesn't mean he doesn't have the same tendencies as those who hurt them. Black people can discriminate against whites, Jews can discriminate against non-Jews, Muslims can hate Christians, and on and on. When we live with expanded empathy, we make few decisions without taking time to ascertain the facts.

4.

Learning to Include or Exclude:
Parental Modeling

*"All my life, I have maintained that the people of the
world can learn to live together in peace if they are
not brought up in prejudice."*

—Josephine Baker

CHILDREN WILL PLAY AND thrive with all others until
someone tells them not to. Prejudice is learned through
a child's early relationships. Within these relationships,
especially with mother and father or whomever the
primary caregivers, modeling is extremely influential
to a child's mind. As we have discussed, children are
not born with negative ideas about themselves or those
they encounter. **Prejudice is learned, and prejudicial
ideas and beliefs can be unlearned.** As children age,
peer groups can have significant influence, however
negative stereotypes can usually be overcome through
parental intercession. Adolescence is a more difficult
time for adults to influence teens regarding peer group
beliefs, but it is still possible.

A professor of education who consults to several
highly-rated public high schools in Massachusetts
recently told me that despite establishing diversity

groups, the schools rarely attract students who are not minorities. These groups are mainly comprised of those who encounter little interest from the greater student population. The consultant also hears racial and homophobic slurs on a regular basis. Whether in high schools or elementary and middle schools, the consensus of what educators are observing is similar. The words "fag," "homo," and "retard" are often heard, as well as other slurs. On the other hand, my daughter Alaina, a kindergarten teacher, says she never hears prejudicial language in her diverse classroom. On Martin Luther King Day, Alaina's colleague, Karen, tells her kindergarten class on how prejudice existed when she was growing up. "Imagine if you couldn't ride on the school bus because you had blond hair or blue eyes? When I was your age, black people had to ride at the back of the bus, or not at all!" A little boy raised his hand to ask a question. "Mrs. McCaw, were you black when you were our age? And then you turned white?"

The innocence inherent in young children is pure and pervasive. However, as these children mature, teachers begin to notice changes. Ideas that they would not have developed on their own begin to emerge.

In a study published in the *Journal of Personality and Social Psychology* seven experiments showing 950 participants photographs of white and black faces was conducted. Non-black subjects judged the black men to be more muscular, stronger and more likely to cause physical harm than the white men, even though both groups were the same in height and weight. Black participants saw the black men as more muscular and strong, but not capable of causing physical harm.

In 1966, *Newsweek* published a study surveying 800 teenagers throughout the United States. The study sought to understand what teens really thought and felt. Fifty years later, *Newsweek* researchers decided to find out what if anything had changed in young people's minds, and Harris Poll was hired to question over 2,000 teens from the ages 13 to 17. The teens came from diverse geographic areas and equally diverse backgrounds. Teens who said that they had faith in God had changed from 96% in 1966 to 83% in 2016. In 1966, 44% thought racial discrimination was a problem; in 2016, 82% thought discrimination was prevalent in their generation. In 1966, 33% thought that discrimination was inevitable; by 2016 number had increased to 91%.

Even though the sixties were a turbulent time for race relations, we still see concern among black teens that they will not enjoy the opportunities given to white teens. By the year 2060, minorities (non-Caucasian) are expected to comprise the majority of the population, so are we to expect discrimination to be prevalent in all walks of life?

Safety and Prejudice

Human beings want to belong; and adolescents especially want to belong. Being prejudiced can provide immediate connection and can make an otherwise insecure person feel safe. As we saw in chapter two through the case of a young man who became attracted to the white supremacy movement, the more disenfranchised a young person feels, the more vulnerable he is to being drawn into a group that strengthens its hold on members through prejudice to a particular race or religion (or toward several other groups whose ideas differ from their particular credo).

In years past, perhaps gay and lesbian youths faced the greatest and often most cruel prejudice; now, transgender and gender-fluid groups that experience more mental and physical abuse than their gay and lesbian peers.

Parental awareness is critical in helping young people avoid gravitating to circles of friends that promote exclusiveness and avoid if not object to diversity. Parents spend more time with their children today as in the past. Fathers have tripled time spent with their children since 1965, although mothers still spend about twice as much time with their children as fathers.

Poor Modeling/High Child Anxiety

Libby is the 36-year-old mother of three-year-old Abby. Her husband John, age 40, works at home while Libby is a part-time aerobics instructor.

Libby recently told me that Abby is crying more and is having a difficult time sleeping.

She also described incidents of fighting with her husband. She says that he slanders her in the heat of the argument, while she screams to be left alone, all in the presence of Abby. John has called Libby a retard, an Irish drunk and a homo lover, as one of her best friends is a lesbian. He has threatened to pull Abby out of day care, as one of the teachers is a lesbian. I have met John, and he seems unlikely to change. He blames Libby for all their conflicts, even for his prejudicial outbursts. Libby understands that her daughter is exposed to intense anger, which is creating anxiety and contributing to her insomnia.

This type of marital dynamic will likely cause the child to feel increasingly insecure. Libby has the difficult role of making sure that Abby does not take on her father's views, but even if she is successful, the anger alone will likely affect Abby. The correlation between growing up in a household full of aggression and anxiety and later depression in adolescence is significant.

John is a biased, angry man. He characterizes others negatively and then steadfastly defends his point of view. On many levels his thought process seems bizarre, yet I have encountered such rigid thinking many times in my career.

We have established that the beliefs expressed within a person's family either initiate the process of prejudice and exclusion or the mindset of openness and inclusion. Children need at least one rational adult to provide a clear and truthful view of the world. In Libby's case, I am sure she will be the parent that her daughter can rely upon to remain open to the world. She is, nevertheless, more likely to fear or even avoid those her father condemns.

So how do we develop the courage to assert our views in the face of prejudice? Many adults struggle to speak out when they hear racial or anti-Semitic remarks. The fear of conflict tends to make people withdraw or remain silent. But we cannot afford to stay silent if we are to create a more just world. On the other hand, attacking those who spew prejudice is not a model that is either effective or sustainable. **Learning to address false statements with tact and assertiveness is certainly an art.** Ask yourself how many adults you know personally who are able to conduct themselves in the face of conflict in this way? Certainly, children cannot learn this approach without teachers or mentors who display the ability that many leaders in our world seem to lack. They need to see effective behavioral responses to slurs and insults. Abby needs to see her mother react to her father differently. If he continues to be defensive and insulting, she must try to assert herself without anger and then, if the intensity increases, she must divest in order to protect herself and Abby. Fighting back is a lose/lose proposition when the other person is unreasonable and highly emotional. Libby's self-esteem is so battered that it has left her depleted and doubtful. Her self-worth has been diminished within the dynamic of the marriage, and when insulted she believes she can't help but fight back and ultimately beg him to stop. I never recommend complete withdrawal without a response, so saying something like '*I am not going to talk to you until you calm down and speak without insulting me*' is appropriate.

Empathy, the capacity to understand and respond to the unique experience of another, teaches us when to invest and when to divest. When situations become volatile, particularly when children are present, it is time to move away. One of the difficulties in teaching when to address a person and when to divest is factoring in an individual's tendency to be conflict avoidant. Individuals often fall into one of two categories when facing conflict. They are either too aggressive (often males), or too passive (often though not always females).

It is difficult to maintain intimacy or deep connections without learning how to effectively manage conflict.

Outside the home, we also see in our political and corporate world many examples of poor interpersonal skills. How outstanding it is when we witness a person in authority managing criticism with curiosity and thoughtfulness. A person who is not defensive when criticized does not strike back but responds with what he or she believes to be the truth. And how refreshing it is when we see an authority figure weigh the evidence and apologize if he or she recognizes that criticism to be accurate. Such people are secure enough to be vulnerable. They are secure enough to not deny reality. These are the characteristics of a soulful parent, educator, politician, theologian or coach, and they can make a tremendous impact on young people.

5.

The Courage of the Young: An Open-Hearted Approach to Diversity

"We need to give each other the space to grow, to be ourselves, to exercise our diversity. We need to give each other space so that we may both give and receive such beautiful things as ideas, openness, dignity, joy, healing, and inclusion."

—Max de Pre

IT IS WELL KNOWN among educators that diversity in the classroom has multiple benefits. Research from Teachers College Columbia has found that K-12 students exposed to peers unlike themselves leads to improved cognitive skills, improved critical thinking and improved problem solving. Students today are growing up in a diverse society, for the first time in our history students of color are now the majority in grades K-12. It is necessary for children today to expand their empathic skills so that they can understand and learn from those who at first glance seem different than themselves.

Psychologist Jaana Juvonen of UCLA studied middle school students in working-class neighborhoods that contained Asians, blacks, whites and Latinos. She and her team found that as diversity in the classroom increased, students on whole indicated that they felt safer, more secure and less likely to victimize children of other races or ethnicities.

Teacher diversity in the US is not keeping pace with the diversity of the greater student body; a majority of teachers in the United States are still white and are educated in mostly white colleges. Retention and recruitment of minority teachers needs to occur, and white teachers must begin to reassess the way they teach. I have spoken with several white teachers in recent months, and although there seems to be a reluctance to admit to not wanting school demographics to change, it is apparent to me that the addition of Latino and black children is still met with an anxiety that, if not acknowledged, could interfere with the grand opportunity that diversity can bring to students and faculty alike. One veteran teacher I interviewed said that faculties are generally supportive of diversity, but parents in affluent towns are more in favor of Indian and Chinese students entering the schools because they expect these children, as a result of their parents' emphasis on education, to advance the school's academic standing on whole. She did say that she does not see the same enthusiasm from parents when black or Latino students enroll.

This bias has led to the label **Modern Minority Myth,** essentially a stereotyping of Asian Americans while making little distinction between Chinese, Japanese, Korean, Vietnamese, Hmong or Filipino children. This has created inordinate pressure for Asian children, possibly a reason that Asian girls have more suicidal thoughts than white girls, and Asian girls between the ages of 15 to 24 have suicide rates 39% higher than their white peers.

It is not only white teachers who fear integrating schools, but white students brought up in homes where prejudice is present can victimize black teachers, discouraging them from being a part of a white majority school. I was recently speaking with a high school teacher regarding her thoughts after reading my previous book, *The Soulful Leader*. She commented that all educators should read the book, and I told her how I was working on a new book on diversity.

She then told me that one of her colleagues, a black teacher named Rosa Slack, was forced out of her job at Kennebunk High School by racist threats that resulted in a court case. She said that Rosa was one of the most compassionate and competent teachers she had ever met. The Kennebunk High School student body is 92% white, with only 1% black and Latino students. Rosa was hired in 2015, only the second black faculty member in the school's history. She had been an educator for 20 years, serving in various teaching and administrative roles. She accepted the role of history teacher at Kennebunk High thinking her position would be ideal for her son who has developmental and physical disabilities. During her short stay one student threatened to burn down her house. A friend of his came to her class with a large Confederate flag draped over his back with the word 'Redneck' written in the center of the flag. One of the students in question had told a peer when he was in middle school that he wanted to "kill all the black people in the school." I can't help but wonder if these boys had also learned gender discrimination. Would they have been so brazen if their teacher had been a black man? The court case that followed centered on Rosa's assertion that her fears were not addressed by administration and that she was discriminated against by receiving below proficient ratings for the first time in her 20-year career.

The shining light of the situation is that the community and the student body overwhelming supported

Rosa. One member of the Board of Directors comple-
mented Rosa's bravery and stated that she was horrified
to hear of the confederate flag being worn in the school.
Community members demanded accountability and
over 30 students developed their own proposal for an
equality action plan. The students' comments were
powerful, essentially pleading with parents to denounce
prejudicial acts, behaviors and words at home.

Children observe social norms early in life. Explicit
and implicit views are internalized at younger ages
than most parents realize. Child psychologists have
conducted research that indicates that bias begins as
early as kindergarten. Children absorb cultural norms
quickly; racial attitudes are internalized as well as sens-
ing which groups or genders are held in higher esteem.
The good news is that these early belief systems can
be changed when young children and adolescents are
exposed to authority figures that help them understand
which cultural biases are not accurate or truthful.

A retired principal who worked in a middle school
with a majority of African American students told me
a story that points to the value of openness of white
educators in a black world. She mentioned that when
she began as principal, the students and parents were
organizing a conference to increase educator awareness
in the community. She commented to the parents,
"You people have done wonderful work." When she
returned to her office the next day she received a call
from her superintendent who told her that the board
of trustees wanted to fire her. Parents had called members of the board complaining about racial overtones
in her words. She immediately apologized to her black
colleague who was overseeing the project. Her fellow
teacher and friend knew her intent was not to hurt but
to compliment. She did, however, also explain that
the phrase "you people" had been used historically to

discriminate. She appreciated the feedback and the learning began. Over the next eight years she became one of the most successful principals in the district, primarily due to her openness to learning and to her humble desire to help her students thrive.

The following example describes the same sense of openness but from a student's perspective in a school system that promotes diversity akin to what my principal friend created in her school.

Did You Know Osama? Correcting Islamophobia myths

I recently read a story about a PBS special called "Stories from the Stage" which featured stories depicting diversity in America. Ironically, the story in question featured a young Muslim man, Furquaan Syed, from my hometown of Hopkinton, Massachusetts. I watched Furquaan's video and was so impressed by this young man's poise and insight that I asked his school superintendent, Dr. Carol Cavanaugh, if she would ask him if I could speak with him about his views on growing up Muslim in the current society.

One Saturday morning, Furquaan and I met, and my major takeaway was that I found myself wishing every American, young and old, could possess the open heart and clear mind that this young man displays. Furquaan had first become aware of prejudice while in the third grade, and then more poignantly when Osama bin Laden was killed. "Kids would come up to me and ask me if I knew him, did I feel sorry for his children because they had lost their father." Furquann realized at that moment that he had been selected as a de facto representative of terrorists who, as he said, had committed heinous acts.

As I was sitting with this handsome, articulate young man, who was so erroneously associated with such despicable acts, I couldn't help but notice that his speech was gentle and thoughtful with no anger. On several occasions he mentioned how grateful he felt to be living in New England, and to be in a high school that "is all about equality, diversity, acceptance and being open-hearted." His focus, rather than being centered on retaliation, was clearly more on understanding and educating those friends who seemed misguided. Furquaan told me that he had spent his early years involved in a local Mosque. Furquaan's father was the outreach representative of this mosque, which he and an imam had developed. This close community gave Furquaan a deep sense of his religion, and also how to navigate prejudice without developing hatred and resentment.

Furquaan expressed two insights he found to be consistently true: parents of young children have far more influence on their children's potential prejudice than their peers; and that even though kids from diverse backgrounds can be friends at school, but if their parents have biases, it will eventually limit or end their friendship over time. He also believes that his generation is the first not to be exclusively influenced by their parents' beliefs. "My friends and I value what our parents think, but in the end we search for the facts and then make our decisions." He told me of conversations that he and his friends have had that are not necessarily representative of any particular religion or ethnic group, but instead of their unique perspectives. They were, for instance, recently discussing their personal views of God, and they took a deeper step into the depths of their beliefs, moving from the general to their own unique beliefs. I mentioned to Furquaan that, from my perspective, his process is at the heart of empathy, as empathy listens, gathers information and only concludes when the facts are clear. He was delighted to know that his generation, according to numerous studies, seems to be the least prejudiced in recent times.

Assimilation; not Isolation

At the conclusion of our talk I asked Furquaan if I might speak with his father. I wanted to understand how he and his wife had raised such a wonderful human being. Also, I was curious about his experience as an Indian Muslim—I already knew he was the outreach representative of a mosque that he and an imam had developed in a city with few Muslims.

Mynuddin came to my office the following Saturday. Like his son, he was a handsome man with an obvious quality of grace and humility, as well as exceptional intelligence. He was optimistic, particularly concerning the United States. He had come to America from South India nearly 20 years ago, and he was aware that Americans need to accept diversity in order to reduce hate crimes. He told me he was aware of the current social climate but believed that Americans are inherently just and would eventually embrace diversity to a greater degree. He gave several examples of people of all faiths supporting Muslims, particularly when there was a ban on Muslims from certain regions in the world entering the country.

He told me that he believed that both sides were to blame for the lack of assimilation. And of course he was aware of damaging stereotypes of Muslims, Jews and those of color. But, he also accents the tendency of particular groups, including Muslims, to resist mixing with the general population. We talked of the natural inclination to remain within our own tribe, but also of the need to go beyond simply relating to those who look and believe as we do, without which the cohesiveness of our own group can become too extreme and too protective. Without familiarity, we are more likely to retain stereotypes. And as a result, we can become isolated, resulting in even less integration as both sides adhere to their erroneous beliefs. The root of this type of tribalism is the insecurity to encounter those who are unfamiliar, and also those that we have been taught to fear.

Mynuddin has tried to encourage Muslims to interact with those of other faiths and ethnicities. When he encounters resistance from those who want to remain within their religious identities but come to America to make a better life for their families, he says to them, "You can't want their money but not their people." We discussed our mutual efforts to expand diversity and he referred me to another video of Furquaan talking to a group after the Muslim ban at the Amazing Things Arts Center in a program called Fugitive Stories, which focuses on storytellers who challenge their audiences with profoundly personal stories. Together, we listened to this young man, who was 14 at the time, and I could not help but tear. The PBS video and the Arts Center Videos are short, please take a few minutes to watch and you will understand why I am so very impressed with Furquaan and with his dad.

You can watch Furquaan's PBS talk at: facebook. com/StoriesfromtheStage/videos/295633624294808.

You can watch the Arts Center video at: https://www. youtube.com/watch?v=3wVbbkwb0tU&t=0h22m45s.

6.

Sinister Shame: Can bad feelings that lead to bad behavior be changed?

"If you really, truly, genuinely care about the people around you, then throw away all that vengeance and hatred, and say to yourself, 'No one shall have to feel what I have felt—no one shall have to bear the pain that I have borne—not on my watch.'"

—Abhijit Naskar

BILLY'S CHILDHOOD LEARNING, LIKE that of so many others who are taught to hate, strongly suggests the conclusion that diversity is spurned based on irrational beliefs about others. That unfortunate circumstance, or attitude, is born out of insecurity and implanted in a young person's psyche at a impressionable time. Billy learned early that achievement and projecting a perfect image provides temporary self-esteem.

With our tremendous emphasis in the United States on appearance and status, what I call *performance addiction*, it is not unlikely that our obsessive need to achieve status has led to an unhealthy society. (In the recent *Bloomberg 2019 Healthiest Country Index* the US was rated at number 35 on the list, with Spain, Italy and Iceland being rated in the top three for overall health.)

We know that prejudice causes anxiety and stress, and also creates brain changes that reduce creativity, productivity and profitability in business endeavors. In personal relationships it creates a sense of distrust and alienation.

In virtually all *Fortune 500* companies diversity training is provided for employees. A recent comprehensive study featured in the *Harvard Review* (7/19) sought to collect data to determine the effects of diversity programs. The authors noted that few programs collected data to determine effectiveness, while noting that even if positive results were initially attained, they did not seem to be sustained. Here are a few notable results from the study:

1. Very little evidence was found that diversity training affected the behavior of men or white employees overall—traditionally the two groups who have the most power in organizations.

2. The training caused women to be more proactive about their own advancement.

3. The training had positive effects on US employees' attitudes and behaviors toward racial minorities. American employees who took the training were more willing than their counterparts in the control group to acknowledge their own racial biases, provide informal mentorship to racial minorities, and recognize the excellent work of their peers who were racial minorities.

The training had a positive effect on the attitudes of employees who were the least supportive of women prior to training. The single largest behavioral effect generated by the training was on the behavior of women in the company's US offices. The training did not prompt men to nominate more women, nor did it lead senior women to nominate more junior women.

Additionally, in 2015 the *New York Times* concluded a study which indicated that there were more CEOs named John running 1,500 companies than there were female CEOs. The study also found that 72% of senior executives were white. The study concluded that despite diversity and inclusion training, people of color and women still find it difficult to rise to executive levels in leadership positions.

What Limits Diversity Efforts?

One reason diversity training may be limited in its effectiveness is that most programs are not continuous. You cannot expect prejudices that have been inbred for years to dissipate by a few sessions that encourage openness. The Harvard study involved two one-hour sessions and a one-hour control group. The reason Billy was able to make a successful change was because the group he belonged to met every week for 90 minutes with the same individuals. The continuity of this approach made it far more effective in eliminating bias toward oneself and others compared to short efforts that have no follow through, and do not benefit from the development of relationships of trust and generosity. Group experiences produce positive brain changes and thus lessen the tendency to be defensive and single minded. Once trust is established, which takes time in any relationship, openness to alternative points of view can take place.

From Shame to Acceptance

I have been conducting leadership and communication groups for over 35 years and I can confirm that Billy's story is typical. On the other hand—and this fact is always incredibly hard for me to accept—there are individuals whose sadism is so entrenched in their character that change seems unlikely. I can count on one hand the individuals I put in this category after treating thousands of individuals. However, they do exist, and when they are in positions of power they can inflict enormous psychological, physical and spiritual pain.

Abuse demeans people and makes them feel inferior. They tend to internalize the abuse on some level and see themselves as lacking in some way. Maybe they are not smart enough, or not pretty or handsome enough, or not athletic enough. And despite the fact that many adults realize that they were treated inappropriately, their feelings, which are recorded in the emotional center of the brain, stubbornly persist. Our thinking brain gives us the facts; our emotional brain may say otherwise.

My family and I vacation on the Southern coast of Maine in summer. I love the magnificence of the sea. I am not a good swimmer, but I can swim. Nevertheless, I never go into the water over my head.

When I was a child of six or seven, I almost drowned in the ocean. Later, I was thrown into the water by a sadistic instructor.

When I was in high school, the kids would go swimming in summer, but I would join one athletic team after another, playing baseball in the afternoon and tag football at night—anything to avoid the water!

I know intellectually that I won't drown, but the old feelings generated by my initial experiences with water persist. It's not rational, it's emotional.

For years, I felt ashamed of my fear of the water. I have worked hard to change my feelings from shame to acceptance of the conditions to which I was exposed.

Years ago, I was treating a Catholic priest from a Catholic university where he taught the religions of man. In his class he was noted for being open, dispelling

40

the ideas that made little rational sense in all the major religions. At the time, the Vatican had just changed its stance on not eating meat on Fridays. It was suddenly alright to do so, even though both my priest client and I had grown up believing it was a mortal sin to eat meat on Friday. Mortal sins, to Catholics, are the most egregious sins.

In one session he commented that he was discovering more and more about emotional conditioning early in life and how hard it is to change our feelings even though we come to realize that such conditioning is not the truth. He mentioned that the origin of not eating meat on Friday came from a Pope, who at the time knew that the meat in Europe was bad and wanted to limit consumption to protect the people. The edict did not come from God, it was man-made, and subsequently undone by man, too. As he was leaving our session, he paused at the door to the waiting room, smiled and said, "I'm still not eating meat on Friday; the facts have not yet overcome my feelings." I knew exactly what he meant. When we come to understand the origin of our learned behavior, and when we accept how difficult it is to change behavior that is accompanied by deep embedded emotion, we are in a position to trade shame for acceptance.

7.

The Fear of Difference: Poor Relationship Skills

"If we cannot now end our differences, at least we can help make the world safe for diversity."

—John F. Kennedy

THE ABILITY TO RESOLVE conflict assertively, directly and tactfully is one of the greatest abilities any human being can possess. Think of how many adults you know who have developed this interpersonal skill to the extent that they can cope with difference without defensiveness and at the same time can present the facts as they know them to be while being open to change. Their goal is to live by the truth rather than being preoccupied with being right.

Calm Listening: What Gets in the Way?

We all know that those who truly listen create trust and openness in others. Those who listen empathically usually possess a sense of calm that relaxes others and, in the process, calm listening changes brain chemistry in a positive way, creating a desire from both parties to be forthcoming. So what interferes with this process?

We know that in order to appreciate and understand others we must be open to diversity. We also know through credible studies at MIT and other universities that diversity in the workplace increases profits. A diversity of personalities produces a diversity of ideas. A study at the University of Virginia School of Business further explored the effects of class diversity as it pertains to success. Those who had lived in different socioeconomic classes at different times were most successful in understanding and communicating with others.

A second study by The American Psychological Association found that those from higher socioeconomic classes tend to over inflate their abilities, often allowing them to fool others into thinking that they are more capable than they actually are.

In my experience, people who are overly impressed with themselves make poor team players and are generally poor listeners. They tend to be dismissive of those below them and are far more deferential to those in power than to peers.

In contrast, the anxiety of those who are self-critical makes them also listen with half an ear. If one is preoccupied with impressing others, or fears that he will not be perceived as good enough, both behaviors compromise the ability to listen effectively. Not all, but many people who grow up in less advantaged situations have difficulty projecting confidence even though the APA study indicated that they perform just as well in testing situations as the colleagues from a higher social class. The less advantaged have not had the same exposure as those in higher classes; they are not inferior but have simply had fewer mentors and experiences.

Barry's story

Barry is 46 and is the father of two preadolescent girls.

He recently joined one of my groups. He describes himself as handsome, bright and underappreciated in the corporate world. He told us that he often skips the line in restaurants and convinces hostesses to allow him to enter ahead of others. At one point, one of the female members told him that he was certainly not the most handsome man in the room. He looked at me, smiled in a coy way, and said, "I understand, Dr. C., that they just can't admit it because they are all so self-critical that they can't stand someone like me who is brimming with confidence."

Barry tells his wife what to wear, critiques her body and clothing often, all in an effort, he says, "to improve her self-image." He has little awareness of his arrogance and little awareness of how poor his relationship skills are as a result. He is five feet seven inches tall, average looking, intelligent but not brilliant as he would claim, and as a result of his narcissism he cannot connect with anyone for long, except those similar to himself. He is either preaching to the choir or not involved. Barry won't admit that he is defensive; he hides behind a false self that protects him from any view of himself that would tarnish his image. His fear of difference and conflict are as significant as the group members who are tormented by self-doubt.

Anxious people have difficulty being present because they are so afraid of being humiliated or demeaned. Narcissistic individuals often fool others by constantly praising themselves, often distorting their achievements altogether. They can make an anxious person even more anxious, and their audiences are usually made up of self-doubting individuals who have bought into the display of narcissistic grandiosity as being real.

Both types of individuals fear difference. One is threatened by anyone who does not idealize and compliment him. The other is threatened before a conversation begins, assuming that they will not be able to hold their own in conversation and not be competent enough to hold another's interest.

Too anxious to hear—too anxious to love

If we are taken away from being in the moment by our conditioning, whatever the source of our internal negatively, we likely to fear difference and only feel comfortable when we know for certain that we are liked and accepted. When we encounter novelty, such as a different look, a different way of speaking, a different religion, or a different nationality, a threat is mistakenly perceived. Most people are anxious to some degree when presented with a unique or unusual situation or circumstance. This is quite normal. Ironically, an opportunity is knocking at our door.

The origins of inclusion are clear

I watch our five-year-old granddaughter Carmela approach other children as they play on the beach in Southern Maine. Carmela, named after my mother, has received so much love and compassion in her early life that she approaches others easily and without anxiety. She will approach children five or more years older and ask, "Do you want to play with me?" The other day she approached two teenage sisters playing soccer. My daughter and I thought surely they would not comply, but they did include her and later swam with her and went out of their way to say goodbye to her at the end of the day. Yesterday she approached a boy who looked to be about eight years old. His reply to the same question she'd posed to the two girls was, "Leave me alone." Carmela simply walked away and said, "What a grumpy kid," then found someone her own age to play with. Her resilience is well developed and strong even though she is young.

Carmela has not only been given abundant love but has also been given appropriate limits so that she respects her parents and others when necessary.

I enjoy listening to Carmela create stories which reveal so much of her inner life and learning. She created a song which she sings often to "bad guys." It goes something like this: "You were not born bad, it's just because of what people did to you; you can become good, just play with me and I will teach you; it's better to be good than bad."

My philosophy exactly!

Just like Billy in our earlier example, **exposure to goodness promotes goodness. It is what I call a goodness breakthrough**.

My daughter teaches in a system in which the students from various cultures—Indian, Chinese, Hispanic—and also several different religions. She tells me that they all play with each other, the boys as affectionate and as empathic as the girls. She also observes that as they age beyond elementary school, their conditioning begins to emerge. Boys become less empathic, and most unfortunate is that children become programmed to remain within their tribe, to the exclusion of others who at one point in their young lives did not seem so different but now are perceived as such. But not in all cases: children who have open-minded parents who integrate rather than segregate are subjected to and guided by the richness of diversity that lies within these examples.

8.

Pathological Certainty: Closed Door to the World

"It is time for parents to teach young people early on that in diversity there is beauty and there is strength."

—Maya Angelou

PATHOLOGICAL CERTAINTY IS AN aspect of a person's character that does not allow for the individual to be wrong or have doubts. They take stands on issues or about people without credible facts and refuse to alter their position despite information that proves their positions are incorrect. This type of person is next to impossible with whom to negotiate, and when combined with a sadistic core, they are the worst people to be in positions of leadership. They are controlling, incredibly insecure and often have little empathy for others. They influence through aggression and fear rather than through high level interpersonal skills and strategic thinking. They are not rational but dogmatic in their thinking and in their actions.

Not all who are plagued by pathological certainty are sadistic but the combination of the two qualities is quite common. They frighten people with their unwavering opinions and attract followers who are as narrow minded as they are or are naïve in their understanding of complex dynamics. They also tend to suffer from performance addiction—the belief that achieving status and perfecting appearance will bring respect and love from others. They are quite driven and competitive and often cannot tolerate any criticism without striking back rather than learning from the contractive feedback of others.

A sure way of accessing a person's sense of self is to view how they respond to criticism.

A secure person may feel slighted initially, but if the criticism is delivered with tact and out of concern, they will eventually access the feedback and learn from the information that they are given, even when it differs from their own assessment of themselves or of issues important to them.

In contrast, individuals who embody pathological certainty will fight against any feedback that offends their sense of self. They do not have the resilience or faith in themselves to take in information from any source other than themselves. They love to be idealized, and when their mask comes off, like the Wizard of Oz, they end the relationship, or those in power may even fire those who stop aggrandizing them.

The Case of a Fragile Boy

Some time ago I was treating a single mom of two adult children. Her daughter, the oldest at 22, became a schoolteacher and was the pride of her mother's life. Her son, age 20, had been acting out since the age of 12, when his alcoholic father left the family. They lived in inner city Boston, in a section that was mainly comprised of black and Latino children. Brian, chubby and quite short for his age, was picked on mercilessly while on the bus, as he was one of a minority of white kids traveling daily to his school.

Brian quit high school at age 16 and moved to Florida to live with his father's brother, also an alcoholic. His uncle introduced him to the white supremacist movement and Brain felt that he had finally found a home and an enemy at the same time. He drank with his uncle and other white nationalists as he was indoctrinated into the movement. His mom asked me if I would see him when he was scheduled to be home for a visit. When I met Brian he was dressed in black, baggy jeans with several chains around his neck, his ears pierced with large rings. During the course of the interview he told me that he and his buddies had beaten Jews and blacks to the point of knocking their victims unconscious. Hatred was in his eyes, and he felt complete justification for hating these "animals that were destroying our country." Brian clearly indicated that he harbored no doubts about his viewpoint, despite evidence that exposed his beliefs to be without foundation.

Evolutionary psychologists believe that all humans have the capacity for evil and for empathy. They cite survival as being the determining factor as to which traits come to the forefront and which remain dormant.

Studies of identical and fraternal twins indicate that our genes contribute one third to possibly one half of the variables accountable for empathy. The remaining percentage is due to what parents and other authority figures contribute to a young person's development.

We also know from credible research that there are two types of empathy. Emotional empathy is experienced immediately, without premeditation. Cognitive empathy, on the other hand, is a rational thought process that is learned from teaching and modeling by parents and other adults to whom children are exposed during very impressionable years. When this experience is not provided, as in Brian's case, psychopathic behavior is more likely to develop. Rather than Brian having adults who modeled compassionate behavior, he had a father and an uncle who modeled cruel, prejudicial behavior. Brain's mother is compassionate, but he rejected her and aligned himself with his dad, as his father blamed his mother for most of his difficulties. Brain learned to blame and be self-righteous early in life. He learned to take pride in certainty, seeing this stance as a strong masculine quality. Ironically, he never learned that expressing doubt or vulnerability could be perceived as strength, and he did not understand that his father and his uncle suffered from feelings of inadequacy. Their defense against their fragile sense of self-worth was grandiosity, or by blaming an enemy and pretending to have all the answers to life's complex questions.

Can Evil Turn to Good?

People who are willing to inflict harm on others tend to be fragile and authoritative and they place more emphasis on stereotypes than on the individual's character or internal makeup. Brian believed that Jews and blacks created their own difficulties and deserved the fate that he and others inflicted upon them. Brian's blind obedience to his uncle and his new cult friends required him to not question the reasoning of those he idealized. It was as if he had no responsibility for his actions, and he is just being directed to harm for righteous reasons, to help white people resume their dominance of the world, and not allow anyone outside their tribe to ruin our country.

Research has indicated that even people who lack emotional empathy—particularly if individuals are exposed to mentoring and modeling that provide ways of understanding and expanding empathy— they can still learn cognitive empathy. Expanding cognitive empathy reduces impulsivity and increases thoughtful decision-making. As I explored how Brian felt as a young person, particularly having to face the humiliation of not being able to defend himself, which resulted in him developing intense hate for whomever he perceived as a perpetrator, he began to soften emotionally. As my empathy opened his hardened heart a bit, he even showed tears as he recalled being alone and without a protector. His fragility, for one brief moment, was exposed. I had the sense that if we had more time he could have worked through his hate and returned to a more stable sense of self. But Brian returned to live with his uncle and eventually, at the urging of his mother, entered a technical program in Florida that earned him an IT certification, which brought him employment. I have only heard that he continues to struggle but drinks less and is easier to relate to when he visits home.

Moving from Certainty to a Love of Diversity

As I have previously indicated, scientists have proven that stressful homes age a child on a cellular level, shortening telomeres, the end of chromosomes that lessen as we age. So they age on an internal level beyond their biological age. There is also a significant correlation between stressful homes and anxiety, depression and addiction in adolescence and early adulthood. A recent study at Massachusetts General Hospital found that family instability can alter a person's gene expression, which can also affect emotional health in significant ways.

Many young people in our current polarized society are searching for ways to feel wanted and connected. Human beings need to connect, and when healthy modeling is not provided for children, adolescents and young adults, then they will find a way to feel better, even if it sacrifices their health in the long run.

In many years of practice I have rarely encountered a patient whose heart could not be opened, particularly if they exposed to or immersed in an environment of people who are empathic, compassionate and listen empathically. All human beings want to be listened to and understood. Many individuals, especially those who suffered difficult childhoods, have never experienced reasonable, caring relationships over a long period of time. Brain chemistry can be changed through empathic relationships. Even one solid adult relationship can make a significant difference to a young person. When this change begins to take place, a person's mind and heart start to open to alternative views other than the ones they have held onto for many years. In essence, such individuals borrow the power of empathy from others to begin to see beyond the surface and into the depth of other's personalities and character. They begin to shed prejudice and ultimately are not so afraid to acknowledge not knowing, or not having all the answers. They also begin to realize that a great burden is lifted when they understand that mature adults often have doubt, confusion and ambivalence. These are normal emotional states; only pretense makes a person think otherwise. As a person feels accepted and understood he becomes more aware of his own emotions, and he also becomes more likely to reexamine beliefs and values. As insight improves, perspectives based on shallow evidence are more likely to be abandoned. The world begins to open, cognitive and emotional empathy expand, impulses decrease as fear is reduced, and a greater sense of awareness of self and of others leads to a desire to be accurate in perception, rather than relying on fixed ideas based on authoritative dogma. In essence, the original fiction story is rewritten to be a nonfiction account of oneself and others.

9.

Uncovering Love: Goodness Breakthroughs

"In choosing a mate, don't pick the tallest and most handsome or the most beautiful. Don't choose one just because that person raises your physical passions. Look for the person who is good from within, the one with substance and worth."

—Helen Quist Milligan

WHEN WE ARE HURT, either in childhood or in adulthood, our emotions can cause us to retreat and then generalize about the person or group who offended us. Many times I have heard individuals in the middle of a divorce make racial, ethnical or gender slurs out of anger. "All men are cheaters." "All women are domineering." One of my clients was thrilled to be marrying a native born Italian. Now in the heat of a contentious divorce, she says, "Italian men are Mama's boys; they are all the same, they cheat, they lie and they go to Mama for consolation. As a wife, you can never live up to their mother's love because the mothers baby them and accept and excuse all bad behavior."

Being Italian myself, I can forgive her statements and smile because I know she is a good woman who is immensely hurt and can't at this time help herself from generalizing. Her statements remind me of my surprise when my mother slurred the Chinese after learning who sold my brother his fatal dose of heroin.

When we are devastated emotionally we can lose our objectivity and our anger can make loving invisible. Much of prejudice is based on learning from distorted sources, but also a degree of prejudice and discrimination is based on our own unresolved hurts.

Can You Forgive or Will You Hold On?

When we think about forgiveness we often think of something we confer on others: *I forgive you.* In truth, we cannot forgive others without forgiving ourselves.

When we deepen our understanding of human nature, our view of the world and of ourselves widens. From this perspective we discover forgiveness for others and for ourselves. Forgiveness is an unfolding process rather than an act that is completed and then set aside. Forgiveness comes slowly, as we continue to learn from the tragedies and traumas of the past in a continual effort to transcend them and return to a positive view of ourselves. With time, determination and effort we move forward, understanding the past rather than endlessly repeating it. This process requires awareness of our own role in whatever difficulty we are experiencing. For instance, my patient Laura had idealized Italian men. She met Lorenzo in Rome on a vacation; she was enthralled with his accent, with the warmth of his family, and with the charisma of his personality, and she made a relatively quick decision to move to Italy. I never met Lorenzo, but I know he had an affair during the first six months of their marriage. She hates him for destroying her dreams, but she is also responsible for her choice.

Perception

Our perceptions are limited by our experiences and by our interpretations of our experiences. Most people who cannot forgive themselves have developed a critical self-voice that holds them to unrealistic expectations. If you have been criticized, ignored or shown little compassion in your life, then you likely have learned to blame yourself for mistakes and errors in judgment. In reality, these temporary flaws simply point to your humanness. On the other hand, some people will go to the other extreme, a place where prejudice and discrimination take hold. Initially, Laura was full of rage toward Lorenzo, and she took little responsibility for her impulsive decision. Then she went to the other extreme of blaming herself. Both positions left out one part being the villain. This black and white, restrictive thinking is what destroys a person internally or destroys their external life, because blaming creates distance and constant friction in a relationship.

People who have grown up with empathy and understanding forgive themselves quite easily when they make mistakes of a small magnitude, because that is the response they received from loving parents and other influential authority figures.

Criticizing vs. Understanding

Every time we demean another person for their imperfections we revisit the times the same behavior was done to us. By repeating this behavior we unfairly punish others for the lack of understanding we received, and in this process we cement our inability to free ourselves and treat others kindly.

In order to forgive oneself, one must turn inwardly and begin to understand how he came to be so hard on himself. Instead of blaming himself for human errors, it is necessary to realize that no child is born with a critical self-voice. The environment that one is exposed can create his demeaning voice, and in time one must seek a more accurate view of himself. Forgiveness arises through the hard work of empathy. In seeking to understand, and opening one's mind and heart to what was once hidden from view, one sees a view of himself that he could not see before, and in that widened perspective, he sees others with the same empathy and open mindedness as he now sees himself.

When we are unable to turn inward, we can become stuck in the prejudicial blaming game. In that frame of reference we reject or even vilify anyone who belongs to the religion, ethnic group or country we felt offended by. The richness of diversity is sacrificed for the membership in one club, an organization of resentful, cut-off and wounded individuals. **Empathy opens the door to the truth, biased thinking and behavior closes all chances of a wider worldview**.

A Goodness Breakthrough

Ironically, kindness toward others is often much easier than kindness toward oneself. When your internal voice is reasonable and fair, your heart opens to the world, and we move outward from self toward others. This new understanding allows us to feel closer to those we previously judged, a defense used in order to create protective distance, and we no longer need to be harsh toward others to shield ourselves.

In forgiving yourself, you forgive others and are far less critical. The world then becomes a kinder, warmer place. Forgiveness now signifies freedom-releasing resentment, bitterness and pride, allowing us to live with ease within, and to love others with uncritical affection. The goodness within each of us is released when we understand and resolve the hurts in our lives. Laura is in the early stages of grief, angst and despair. With the help of others I expect she will return to the giving, compassionate person I know her to be. She will have to let go of holding Lorenzo exclusively responsible for the failed marriage. He violated her trust and is responsible for violating his commitment to his marriage. And Laura will hopefully learn to slow down and use empathy to access others before jumping in with little knowledge of the other person's character. I always say that we learn the most about other people under stress. Laura became enthralled in the romantic city of Rome—understandable but certainly not wise considering the short time they knew each other. Once she heals her broken heart she can return to the giving person she has been in the past.

The Formula for Being Bias Free

In order to perceive accurately we must understand a few basic aspects of human nature. When we are hurt—especially when are deeply hurt—we are prone to generalizations. Once we realize this tendency, it is likely that we can limit ourselves to the facts regarding a hurtful interaction or experience. **No single person represents any entire group**. This is the first step in focusing on actual experience, and the more general we make an occurrence, the more unnecessary work we will have to do later. We create a larger problem than actually exists. Laura will not be well served by hating or fearing all Italians, or whatever ethnic or religious group might offend her in the future. One must focus on the behavior of the person in one's presence, not his entire ethnic, religious or gender group. **Prejudice is born when objective facts are ignored or not understood**.

10.

The Societal Cancer: Sadistic Blaming

"The persecution of Jews in occupied Poland meant that we could see horror emerging gradually in many ways. In 1939, they were forced to wear Jewish stars, and people were herded and shut up into ghettos. Then, in the years '41 and '42 there was plenty of public evidence of pure sadism. With people behaving like pigs, I felt the Jews were being destroyed. I had to help them. There was no choice."

—Oskar Schindler

WHEN I READ OSKAR Schindler's words I wish we all had the depth of empathy he possessed to say "there was no choice." I fear, at some moments, that we have become a desensitized culture. The bombings, the mass killings, the purposeful destruction of temples, churches and innocent children often causes me to wonder how a child living in Syria feels, with disaster looming around every corner. How can these children thrive in such an environment? And yet some do, remarkably. Yet, others adopt the behavior of the killers they encounter; they adapt to cope, to live another day. Renowned child therapist Alice Miller believes that sadism takes years to develop, and is the result of being raised in a hopeless situation. Sadism becomes a way of coping. She believes sadism is the result of pent-up feelings, and of having no acceptable outlet for fear of an aggressive parent's reaction. The destructive nature, if fueled by suffering, needs to repress rather than express.

I agree with her for the most part, however my worry is that I know that a sadistic core to a personality can be so entrenched that trying to treat the sadistic person is like trying to turn cement into liquid again. Sadists tend to blame, they want control and they want to restrict the autonomy of those close to them. They lie to keep their worlds ordered in a way that makes them feel temporarily secure.

Heinz Kohut, the founder of Self Psychology, was the first, to my knowledge, to point out that empathy has a dark side and can be used for sadistic purposes. He noted that when the Nazis attached loud sirens to their dive-bombers, they knew the strange sound would create panic in people on the ground. Using the dark side of empathy, by knowing how to look into the hearts and souls of others, and knowing their thoughts and feelings, the Nazis manipulated the emotions of their victims, creating fear in a pre-meditated manner.

Hitler knew how to use the dark side of empathy. He was quite adept at exploiting the German people's fears of humiliation and poverty as he went into tirades portraying himself as the one who could protect them from evil and bring Germany back to world power.

Kohut's life's work was based on the conviction that sadism, destructive aggression, is not innate but the product of an early environment that is perceived as non-responsive. Sadism can then be viewed as an attempt to protect a fragile sense of self. The sadistic person has never felt valued, accepted, appreciated or truly loved, and the rage that has been held inside will always find a victim, especially when criticized. Any emotional hurt is reacted to with 10 times the force of the slight.

There are contemporary studies that identify brain abnormalities in those who seem to feel little or nothing when they destroy others. Both Timothy McVeigh and Ted Bundy are examples: each suffered significant emotional pain during their childhoods and then held others accountable for their distress.

I agree with Miller and with Kohut, but I would also add that while there may be a difference in the sadist's brain, it does seem that environment determines the expression of the malady by influencing the capacity for manipulation and destruction rather than for love and kindness.

The Origin of Rage

Several years ago, I invited a 34-year-old woman who had emigrated from Greece as a young child to attend one of my group sessions. I met her after she'd made a suicide attempt and was rushed to a local emergency room where it was determined that her attempt was a direct act to get even with her parents. At the time, Alena was five feet two inches tall and quite overweight. She told me that she had struggled with her weight all her life. The psychiatrist she was seeing had prescribed an antidepressant, but after her attempt he declined further treatment, saying that she was obstinate, did not keep appointments and had no interest in using his services to change.

As I got to know Alena, I realized I had seldom encountered anyone with such rage and hatred for so many others. Her prejudices were too numerous to list. Nevertheless, I determined that she had become attached to me, and eventually to group members as well. One reason for those connections was that she enjoyed demeaning and humiliating others. She was an expert at finding the flaw in a person and then using her insight to humiliate and condemn. On several occasions during individual sessions my refusal to hit back when she was insulting me led to important personal revelations. She told me she was raped by an uncle when she visited Greece at the age of 12. She also told me that she was raped in the US at age 19 when she accepted a ride home from a 27-year-old man she had met after a heavy night of drinking. She told me her father was a physically abusive alcoholic who hit all three girls, and she, being the youngest, believed she absorbed the most abuse because she was the only daughter still living at home when they moved to the US, and because both parents had great difficulty adjusting to the new culture. Her older sister had remained in Greece with an aunt, and her other sister lived with relatives in California to make it easier for her parents.

A Temporary Breakthrough

One evening during a group session Alena called another member fat, and said that fat people always seemed to have fat mouths. Of course, we all looked at her with surprise, knowing that she was quite overweight herself. Her statements represented a spontaneous sharing of self-hatred projected onto another person. One of the male members, an older man with handsome features, looked at her with dismay and said, "You probably won't believe me, but I do like you. You are smart, and I know you have suffered greatly in your life; but the one thing I can't stand about you is that you are a sniper—you wait, you calculate, and then you pounce on people. And the worst part is that you enjoy it!"

For the first time when criticized by another member of the group, Alena did not respond. She couldn't hide her reaction as tears welled in her eyes. His opinion really mattered to her. A few weeks later she admitted to me that she had a crush on the man and couldn't believe he saw her in such a negative way.

For several weeks she seemed different. She even made attempts at online dating. In fact, she told the group how excited she was to be dating, and that she had found someone she really liked. After five or six dates she slept with him, and after that experience he never called her back. Her rage and hatred of everyone in her midst returned, yet not quite with the previous force, as group members supported her with compassion and understanding. In effect, the group members became the good guys, and the rest of the world was damned.

You Don't Like Me Because I Hate People

Shortly thereafter, during an individual session, Alena said to me, "You could never be with someone like me because you can't stand that I hate people and that I like to hurt them. You try to be neutral, but when I say awful things about group members, I can see the hurt in your eyes."

Alena was correct, as she often was in her observations of others. I told her how engaging she is when she displays kindness and when she delivers her insights with tact and tolerance. I also agreed that her sadism was hard to tolerate and was the one quality that prevents her from getting close to other people.

Alena continued with group and individual sessions for another year and seldom displayed the sadism that we witnessed regularly in the early days. She had already ended individual meetings, and then, due to a change in her work schedule, she could no longer attend group sessions either. She was scheduled to come to say goodbye to everyone at one last session, but she never appeared and never returned any of my calls. I have always wondered what happened to that broken heart, and always wished she would return to therapy.

Sadistic Leaders

We can see how Alena habitually injured people emotionally; in fact, everyone in the group later admitted that they feared her. But Alena was limited to hurting only those she personally encountered. But leaders who are sadists and blamers can affect thousands, if not millions. Numerous examples throughout history illustrate horrific acts committed by sadistic dictators. Corporate leaders can have the same psychological make-up. Toxic leaders don't usually inflict physical pain, but they can drastically influence the health of employees.

A recent study at the University of Manchester's Business School examined how employees are affected by toxic leaders. They assessed 1,200 workers in a variety of industries from a number of countries. They found a significant correlation between toxic leadership and clinical depression in employees. This type of leader influences an entire business culture, creating an aggressive group who become critical and overly competitive with each other. It is as if they are in a family with a crazy parent, like children who adopt abusive parents' patterns of behavior.

Trust in both business and political leaders is at an all-time low. Sadistic leaders are the worst people to occupy powerful positions; they lack ethics, integrity and authenticity. They use the dark side of empathy to manipulate those they lead, and they enjoy hurting others, which is the absolute worst quality any human being can have. We all hurt each other at times, but usually it is not intentional. Sadistic leaders, sadistic parents, sadistic politicians and even theologians will hurt with joy and impunity if their fragile egos are offended.

Empathy is a great assessment tool; when used properly it helps us know who to get close to and who to remain distant from. We all need to expand our range of empathy—now more than ever.

Expansive empathy allows us to become aware of our own prejudices so we can reexamine false ideas about others. Empathy is not a passive emotion; it needs to be put into action to be effective. When we are confronted with prejudice, sadism, and false beliefs, we need to speak up and to ask questions as to how an individual came to believe distorted facts. Reasonable people will comply; they may be uncomfortable initially but they will want to know the truth because they are people committed to living honest lives. Distortions begin with the awareness that negative and hateful internal dialogue is often projected onto others, and is the most common defense of the sadist.

11.

The Greatest
Prejudice of All: Self Hate

*"There is no such thing as a faithless person; we either
have faith in the power of love, or faith in the power of
fear. For faith is an aspect of consciousness. Have faith
in love, and fear will lose its power over you. Have
faith in forgiveness, and your self-hatred will fall away.
Have faith in miracles, and they will come to you."*

—Marianne Williamson

THE MOST POWERFUL ADDICTION **of all is an addiction
to our own negative thinking.** No one was born with
negative thoughts. We learn negative self-talk through
what we see, how we perceive and how important
people respond to us in our lives. Studies have shown
that the majority of people engage in negative self-talk.
Kamal Chopra of the University of Lethbridge was able
to teach first grade students to rethink and rearrange
self-negativity by helping them identify positive and
negative self-talk. In addition, they were taught how to
convert negative internal dialogue into positive self-talk
while helping them to implement their new learning
into daily interactions. The study displayed that even
at a very young age children can learn to have control

over the inner dialogue that has such dramatic consequences throughout their lives.

Psychologist Ethan Kross of the University of Michigan has conducted several studies to help people reverse
negative self-talk by using a self-distancing perspective.
Essentially, to imagine being outside yourself in order
to observe yourself objectively. He believes that in cases
where people are making difficult decisions they refer to
themselves using their name or by saying "you," "he" or
"she." He cites the Nobel Peace Prize recipient Malala
Yousafzai interview with John Stewart. She was asked
how she coped with knowing the Taliban were plotting
to kill her. "I used to think that the Taliban would come
to kill me. Then I said to myself, 'What would you do,
Malala?' I replied by saying to myself, 'Malala, just take
a shoe and hit him.' She shifted her focus outside herself
for a moment. Dr. Kross believes this change in focus
allows a person to cope more effectively with less stress.

My own approach is a bit different in that I ask
clients to express their negative self-talk out loud in
our group meetings. Of course, this exercise could be
done with a spouse or a close friend. When internal
dialogue becomes external it does seem to provide a bit
more objectivity than when such talk remains internal.
People often laugh when they remark that they are
stupid, ugly, not competent, not skilled at anything,
too old, too fat, too bald, etc. I encourage people to
learn the CD they keep repeating in their minds. We
tend to know the negative things we say to ourselves
quite well. It's like an old CD where we know every
song, every lyric. It has been paved into our brain like
an old highway driven over thousands of times. When
we become aware of the old record we are more able to
press the stop button and move away from whatever
we learned in early development about ourselves that
is actually not factual.

In order to permanently change the effect of negative self-talk we need to share with others our intimate thoughts. We must have the courage to be vulnerable so that we can learn the truth about ourselves from the rational, compassionate people who are in our lives today. When one grows up without empathy, love and understanding, he bases his view of himself on the caregivers in his life. If their view of him is distorted, then so will his self-perception be inaccurate. It's like looking in a cloudy mirror and trying desperately to see how one looks.

If we do not go through this process, then we maintain a compromised view of ourselves. It takes energy to criticize oneself; it changes brain chemistry, producing the stress responder cortisol, with all its negative physical consequences. The sadist projects this accumulated tension outward, while the person with a conscience will more likely internalize negativity with a resultant low mood or even depression.

Old Beliefs Die Slowly

A witty client of mine played a trick on me one session. Jake had left the corporate world to become an addiction counselor and he was taking a course in group psychotherapy to obtain his license. He began one night by telling me that he had a great paragraph from a book he was reading describing the benefits of group therapy. He asked if he could read it to me. Of course I agreed. He read the paragraph, and I told him I was impressed with the insights of the author. Then he asked me if I knew who had made the remarks. I said I did not. He told me that these were my words from my first book, *Treatment of Abuse and Addiction: A Holistic Approach* written in 1998. I instantly felt uncomfortable complimenting myself, and also thought the comments weren't so insightful after all. My old story about myself revealed remnants of the struggle I'd had early on believing that I was competent and intelligent. We both laughed and agreed on how deeply our old views of ourselves seem to be embedded in our minds.

Today I feel differently about myself, but I also realize that those old impressions are still a part of my memory. I remember the hurt and devastation I felt when our guidance counselor told me I was not college material. He handed me brochures from the navy, army, marines and air force and told to talk it over with my family and make a decision. I believed he knew me better than I knew myself. After all, he was the man with a bachelor's and master's degree! I was only a high school athlete who didn't find classes particularly interesting and thus performed the minimum to get by.

Inner Thoughts/Negative Mood

We know that thoughts have an effect on brain chemistry. Negative self-talk produces the stress response, while positive self-talk produces the opposite. With practice we can change our internal dialogue, not easily but with consistent effort we can limit the old inaccurate story that we accept about ourselves.

When my maternal grandmother passed away, my aunt Donna came to live with us. My aunt was in high school when I was in elementary school. She was and still is my second mother, the most compassionate and kind individual one might ever meet. Throughout my childhood I looked up to her. As a young boy, while my parents were at work, I would put my feet on top of hers and she would teach me to dance as we listened to the latest popular tunes. But whenever I complimented my aunt, which was often, she would dismiss my positive comments. As I got older I would ask her to just say 'thank you,' and today she will always say 'thank you' with a wink of her eye as she looks in my direction when others compliment her.

My aunt will tell you today that this little exercise has worked for her. I am not saying that her negative self-talk is eliminated, but the practice of catching her old automatic response has made a difference in her sense of self. Similar to Dr. Kross's work, this method is another way of seeing ourselves more objectively. Group meetings can accentuate this process as members come to know each other, and as the consensus they reach about each other becomes difficult to deny. I know from years of experience that negative self-talk can be changed, and that this change will significantly improve mood and well-being.

What If Self Hatred Remains

The danger of negative self-talk, and particularly self-hatred, is that if it is not altered, then it can result in projecting the hatred outward. Of course this is not true in every instance, but when it is a component of a personality seeking consciously or unconsciously to locate hate in someone else, then it is extremely dangerous.

Alena's hatred of others was an entrenched way of trying to elevate herself by humiliating others. When she joined group sessions she had little awareness of what she was doing. Once she became attached to other members of the group, her hatred lessened and her ability to relate improved. So many others with a similar constitution have not had and will not have this experience.

My particular concern is having individuals with such hatred in positions of power. Whether as heads of families, heads of companies, administrators of schools or God forbid, heads of nations.

12.

A Scary Trend:
The Desentization of Prejudice

"No one is born hating another person because of the color of his skin, or his background or his religion. People learn to hate, and if they can learn to hate they can learn to love, for love comes more naturally to the human heart than its opposite."

—Nelson Mandela

SEVERAL STUDIES HAVE DEMONSTRATED that frequent exposure to hate speech online or in person desensitizes those listening to forms of verbal violence against particular groups. This exposure lessens the perceived suffering of victims and increases prejudice to whatever group is being demeaned.

A study featured in the journal *Aggressive Behavior* verified that hate speech breeds hate and violence. Three Polish professors conducted three experiments focusing on the Muslims and LGBT populations, seen as the two minorities affected most by hate speech in Poland. They randomly selected over 1,000 Polish adults and showed them six examples of verbal violence. They were asked to rate the examples on a seven-point scale, and then they were asked if they would accept members of the Muslim or LGBT community as neighbors, family or co-workers. Their findings confirm that as exposure to hate speech increased, people became less sensitive and were bothered less by it. Basically, exposure to hate speech consistently produced an increase in levels of overt prejudice.

There is no question that prejudice is learned. The good news is that anything that is learned can likely be unlearned.

Denial is the fuel that perpetuates prejudice. Awareness and acknowledgement of a biased view is the beginning of changing a perspective one comes to see as untrue. Individuals who work on changing their internal dialogue from negative to positive are usually the same people that become committed to not only seeing the truth about themselves, but they also are likely to become committed to seeing the truth about others. **Those who have the courage to face the truth about themselves are likely to extend this effort to the world, and understanding how prejudice toward oneself robs a person of happiness creates empathy for others who we know are being objectified for unfair reasons.**

As a young child I dreamed about playing professional football. I would read about and watch football as much as possible. I once asked my father why we never see black quarterbacks, yet they seem to be the best players on most teams. I remember he hesitated and then said, *"Some people think they are not bright enough."* I'm not sure why he said 'some people.' Was he hesitant to acknowledge his own prejudice? Was he conscious of not wanting to create prejudice in his son's mind? Or did he simply not know the answer. As an athlete I was able to answer the question for myself as I played with black athletes and worked out with black friends in college, and through my exposure I saw firsthand that there was no discernible difference in intelligence between white and black players. In fact, in college classes I often thought black students seemed to be more passionate about learning and far more aware of societal issues than those of us who grew up in a more sheltered environment.

Exposure on both fronts makes a difference. My exposure, luckily, in athletics and in college classrooms, dispelled much of what I had heard that was inaccurate about different races and religions. But if I'd had the exposure that Brian or Alena endured, I might have different beliefs today.

Prejudice and discrimination are learned, just as appreciation for diversity and acceptance and joy in engaging those who seem different is also learned. Children are profoundly influenced by the authority figures in their lives; they take in information in the early years with little discernment.

My granddaughter Carmela played with a dark-skinned Indian girl on the beach for several days this summer in Maine and never once mentioned her color. Her parents and Carmela's parents are free of prejudice, so it doesn't exist within their children. I am still a bit surprised when my clients tell me that they feel uncomfortable when their children play with other children of certain races or religion. This is always said with embarrassment, hoping I will not disapprove or think less of the person admitting their biases.

I view these occasions as an opportunity to uncover how certain individuals have learned to fear others who seem threatening for reasons that have never been thoroughly examined. I am always interested in the rationale of these anxieties and fears.

A Feeling is Not a Fact

Our nation, as well as many others, is becoming increasingly diverse. If we are not able to expand our ability to access others based on facts rather than stereotypes, then fear and possibly aggression will proliferate. If we accept that uncomfortable feelings are quite natural when we face novel situations, then we will free ourselves to explore rather than withdraw.

I was extremely fortunate to be watching the great Jewish comedian Jackie Mason in a skit he performed on one of his short-lived comedy shows years ago. He was out on a little deck outside his apartment, I believe in New York City, and he was upset that his neighbor to his right, also on a little deck outside his apartment, wouldn't talk to him because he was Jewish. The monologue went something like this:

"How stupid it is for you to hate me because I am a Jew. You don't even know me, you don't even talk to me, yet you decide I'm no good because I'm a Jew. Now, my wife—she's much smarter than you— she *does* hate me, but she has real evidence. She really knows me. She goes by the facts, not by some silly idea planted in your thick head."

I'm not sure how accurate my memory is about Jackie's performance, but I'm sure you get the point.

A Journey of Truth

If we want to live in our diverse world with ease and joy, we all must reevaluate the ideas we accepted as naïve children observing biased adults. Our future depends on each of us making this effort. Commit to a journey of uncovering the truth about yourself and others, and you will be part of making a world based on compassion for all, rather than a world based on small minded perspectives that limit the potential of many for the favor of a few. The more we encounter others, those who seem different on the surface, the more we find out who we really are!

13.

The Transformation of Beliefs: Empathy Circles and Group Practices

"Opinion is really the lowest form of knowledge. It requires no accountability, no understanding. The highest form of knowledge is Empathy, for it requires us to suspend our egos and live in another's world."

—Bill Bullard

I RECENTLY SPOKE WITH Edwin Rutcsh, founding director of the Center for Building a Culture of Empathy. He has been working for over 12 years to create a more empathic society. He has interviewed over 200 empathy experts and posted the interviews on his website, CultureofEmpathy.com.

Edwin created a simple and accessible method of learning, practicing and deepening mutual empathy in small groups called Empathy Circles. He uses this method to lessen political, social, family and personal divides. He says he finds Empathy Circles to be the most effective first step or gateway practice for enhancing empathy skills.

Family Empathy Circles

Rutcsh has used this practice extensively in mediating family conflicts. (See *Healing a Conflict in My Family* at: http://j.mp/2oMDezu.)

Political Empathy Circles

Edwin has also used empathy circles to mediate between the political left and right. (See http://sites.google.com/site/empathyten/pop-ups/2017-07-02.)

Mediating six pairs of people from the political left and political right, Edwin documented that each mediation ended with a hug between participants and an agreement to do follow-up Empathy Circles online.

Empathy Circles were also conducted on the Los Angeles City Hall lawn. There were approximately 2,000 anti-Trump demonstrators as well as pro-Trump demonstrators. (See http://sites.google.com/site/empathytent/pop-ups/201707-02).

This work is contained in a new documentary called *Trumphobia*. (See the trailer at: http://www.facebook.coom/TrumpphobiaDoc/video/427549897889847/.)

Edwin also facilitates weekly left/right Empathy Circles at: http://www.empathycircle.com/why-paticipate-in-circle.

Edwin's method consists of a structured dialogue to increase mutual understanding and assuring that each party feels heard to its satisfaction. Edwin has had significant success with helping political parties on the right and left understand each other without the typical defensiveness and name calling that has been so common in opposing political gatherings. The following directions are taken from the website CultureofEmpthy.com

How-To: Basic Empathy Circle

An Empathy Circle is a structured dialogue process that effectively supports meaningful and constructive dialogue. It increases mutual understanding and connection by ensuring that each person feels fully heard to his satisfaction.

The Method:

In a circle of three to five participants, 1) The first person selects who they wish to speak to; 2) He/she speaks about whatever suits them for a set time (typically three to five minutes); 3) The listener reflects what he/she is hearing until the speaker feels understood to his/her satisfaction; 4) Then it is the listener's turn to select who they wish to speak to and, for that new listener to reflect what he/she has heard; 5) Everyone must hold the circle process by monitoring and sticking to the steps. The dialogue continues around the circle for the allotted time.

Speaker Tips:

- Pause often to give listeners the chance to reflect on what they have heard.

- When the speaker is finished talking, and he/she feels heard, he/she can say, "I'm fully heard" to indicate that he/she is done with his turn.

Active Listener/Reflector:

- In his own words, the listener can reflect the essence of what he heard the speaker say.

- Each participant must refrain from asking questions, judging, analyzing, detaching, diagnosing, advising or sympathizing. When it's his turn to speak, he can say whatever he wishes to say.

- The listener may ask the speaker to pause periodically so he can reflect on what he has heard.

Silent Listeners:

- All should listen to the exchange between the speaker and active listener/reflector. Each will soon have his turn to actively listen and to speak.

- The group may choose to have a discussion topic or question to address within the circle.

How Group Experiences Enhance Diversity:

As I mentioned earlier, I have led three out-patient group sessions for over 30 years. Each group has a total of 10 (male and female) members, whose ages range from mid-thirties to late seventies. These group sessions are different than Edwin's Empathy Circles in that they are not structured but rather involve ongoing spontaneous conversations between members focused primarily on giving and receiving feedback about each other, based on in-group interactions. Ultimately, we reach a consensus as to an individual's true nature. Members come from all walks of life, different ethnic groups, different or no religious affiliations, and about a third of the members have emigrated to the United States from different countries.

Support groups often enlist those who have similar background or problems. For instance, there may be a group formed for people with teens with anxiety, or adults with drug issues, and so on.

My group's composition is heterogeneous, with the mission of improving perceptions of oneself and others, while bettering the ability to access others accurately through expanding a person's range of empathy. As we understand others and ourselves beyond the surface, we are in a position to relate more effectively in the workplace and are in a better position to know how to maintain intimacy in personal relationships.

For instance, a person may join the leadership and communication group believing that they relate quite authentically and see themselves quite accurately. As they receive feedback to the contrary by others in the group, they often begin to question their original assumptions about themselves. The same process takes place in terms of a member's initial impressions of others. Some impressions turn out to be accurate; some turn out to be far from truthful.

A typical Interaction-Gender Bias, Religious Bias

Frank, a 56-year-old CEO, is a lifelong Episcopalian. He was listening to Mary, a 52-year-old retired high school English teacher, who is an atheist and often offended by people in her life who try to convince her to believe in whatever religion they embrace.

Ling, a 33-year-old Chinese graduate student, is quite outspoken and aggressive. She states that "Most white people try to convince you to be Christian; its like they have never heard of Buddhism."

Frank tries to explain to Mary that he is not judging her, but that he does think she is missing out on a great opportunity. Mary comments, "Maybe you are the one who is missing out by belonging to a cult."

As you might expect, more group members became involved, some subtly taking sides and the more veteran members, those who have worked hard to expand their ability to perceive beyond the surface, continued to follow the facts in the conversation. Jamie, a 36-year-old HR director, comments that she can understand the different sensitivities in the room but, "I don't think we are really listening to each other. People can't wait to speak; let's slow down and try to understand each other's views."

Jamie began her time in the group as conflict-avoid-ant. She grew up in an alcoholic home where her father held prejudices against many people and has always been anti-immigrant even though his grandparents came to the United States from Ireland.

Jamie learned early to be a pleaser, to never object, and to try to just stay safe by appeasing others, for fear of their anger. Over time she has learned to be less fearful and has mastered the ability to be tactfully assertive without anxiety. She has the interpersonal skills to see herself and others accurately. She, by her comments, is guiding Frank, Mary and Ling to slow down and actually listen without the biases that have accumulated within each of them due to past condi-tioning and experiences.

As the discussion proceeded, we eventually dispelled several misconceptions through engaging in non-defen-sive empathic listening and subsequent understanding. People come to this experience with the commitment to become aware of their biases while adopting new perspectives based on objective facts. Regardless of the content of discussions, a consensus is usually reached as to the accuracy of views and/or beliefs. The willingness to let go of conditioning and accept the truth is an integral part of the process.

A few interesting facts

Atheists are not in need of religion to lead altruis-tic, giving lives. The Effective Altruism movement, consisting mainly of atheists, has made significant contributions to charitable organizations. They are committed to personal growth and to the development of the human mind.

Secondly, Americans have become quite aware of Buddhism, which is the third largest religion in the

United States, a 15% increase since 1960. Hawaii and California have the highest percentage of Buddhists. Non-Christian groups are steadily increasing, as the youngest religious groups in the United States are non-Christian.

14.

Me Too Movement Garners Respect for All Throughout the World

"I didn't tell anyone for I think seven years. I didn't know how to think about it, I didn't know how to accept it. I didn't know how to not blame myself or think it was my fault. It's something that really changed my life. It changed who I was completely. It changed my body, it changed my thoughts."

—Lady Gaga

In 2006, Tarana Burke founded the Me Too movement to help survivors of sexual violence recover and heal. Today this movement has spread to 85 countries and has resulted in an acute awareness of what was hidden or denied for centuries. An ABC/*Washington Post* poll discovered that 75% of Americans believe sexual harassment is a problem in our country. Most importantly, the Me Too movement has extended its reach to include stopping harassment of the disabled, LGBTQ individuals, and also those of color.

A survey featured in the *Harvard Business Review* in July 2019 sought to determine if sexual harassment in the workplace had lessened since the Me Too movement reached its height in 2016. In 2016, women taking part in this survey reported being sexually coerced 25% of the time; in contrast, in 2018 the number was reduced to 16%. However, reports of gender harassment increased from 76% of women in 2016 to 92% in 2018. The researchers speculated that obvious sexual harassment has declined while an increase in anger towards women has increased, possibly a reaction to closer scrutiny of sexual harassment. A study published in the medical journal *JAMA Internal Medicine* determined that one in 16 American women's first experience with sexual intercourse was rape, a staggering figure supported by other studies that indicate that 40% of women have experienced sexual violence in their lifetime.

In my clinical experience, men who are hateful toward minorities or toward a particular religion are more likely to harass those of the opposite sex as well. Racism and sexism are often correlated. It is likely that the mindset of a black and white thinker, those with authoritative personalities that make decisions based on good-bad, right-wrong, us-them rigid thinking that does not allow for alternative views. Differences in opinions or beliefs are too threatening to those who crave power and control.

The Women in My Early Life

When I was an undergraduate, my roommates would post pictures of Playboy and Penthouse models all over our apartment. It was embarrassing to me; I actually found pictures of Doris Day and Mary Tyler Moore and posted them in my room. I felt very uncomfortable with the objectification of women. I also didn't want anyone I dated to see those pictures. From an early age I noticed how my mother, my aunt and my grandmother were treated, and I had the same discomfort as I did in that apartment years later. My aunt Donna lived with us after her mother and my grandmother died in her early fifties. My mother always said she died of a broken heart. My grandfather had had affairs and she found one of his lover's letters in his suit jacket and later that day she had a fatal heart attack. My aunt, his daughter and five years older than me, came to live with us. She has a heart as expansive as the ocean and she, as well as my mother and my grandmother, had a profound influence on my life. All three had the ability to be highly compassionate, great listeners and devoted to family. Even though my grandmother passed away when I was very young—I believe I was around eight years old—I have fond memories of her and the conversations we had as she watched over my brother and me when my parents both worked in their small furniture store.

I attended a parochial Catholic school in the elementary years and I did not like the experience. I found some nuns to be overly authoritative and rigid, although not all of them. I would purposely miss the bus, hang out at a local pond, and then return once I knew my mother had left and my grandmother had come to watch us. My hands were often frozen during the winter, and my grandmother would warm them over the stove and plead with me to go to school the next day. Remarkably, I never told my parents about my routine. My grandmother tried to reason with me—I could see the concern in her eyes—and as a result I did return to school because I did not want to hurt her any further.

I remember the day she passed away. My mother and I were visiting her, and when I walked into the room where she was sitting, she rose and said my name in the softest tone. She always spoke in soft tones—I can still recall the warmth of her voice. My aunt and my mother had the same soft tone of concern in their voices. The men in my world back then were good people but tough and often did not display the ability to listen attentively or give as much as they received. These early experiences shaped my view of male/female relationships. I had regret for my mother, grandmother and aunt in that they did not seem to receive much appreciation for their efforts. Male/Female roles were fixed and each gender knew exactly what was expected of them.

If not for my experiences with these three women, I doubt I would have become a clinical psychologist. They taught me how to listen, how to care and how to see beyond the surface. I also learned that I did not want to be in a relationship akin to what I had viewed. My dad loved my mother but he did not use words to express his love, nor was he likely to compliment her and acknowledge how much she did for all of us. By observing what my mother, grandmother and aunt longed for, I was able to realize what was missing in their relationships, and what should have been provided.

Mothers Transfer Sexist Attitudes

Psychologist Maite Garaigordobil and her colleague at the University of Basque Country, Spain conducted studies with 1,455 adolescents and their mothers and fathers to determine how sexism is transferred in attitudes. They determined that the degree of sexism that the mother possesses is more influential to daughters and sons than the influence of fathers. Their work also confirmed that boys and fathers have significantly higher levels of sexism than girls and mothers. Dr. Garaigordobil speculates that mothers are more influential in general than fathers regarding the transference of values, and often spend more time with their children. Consequently, it is assumed that fathers are more pivotal in terms of sexist attitudes.

Other studies have indicated that if stereotypes about girls and boys are embedded (for instance, boys have more status than girls), then as they enter adolescence these stereotypes can lead to boys feeling comfortable making sexual comments to girls and potentially acted inappropriately by feeling that they have the right to touch females without their consent.

Some of the most difficult patients I have ever treated are those who not only verbally abuse their wives, but have been physically abusive to their children. Several had mothers who were demeaning, and accused their sons of not being manly while humiliating them in public. Of course, fathers play a significant role, but as in my own experience, a close mother/son relationship in addition to other significant females makes a tremendous difference in terms of a young boy's view of females.

I Didn't Mean to Hit Her

John, 46 years old and the father of three girls, came to see me for anxiety and to deal with his alcoholic mother and brother as he was constantly pulled into their lives to regulate their drinking. In the first few sessions John seemed quite articulate and overly verbal, meaning he liked to talk and talk without interruption. His desire to be heard was extreme, and he admitted to overreacting whenever his kids, and particularly his wife, would become impatient with his long, rambling explanations of how they had offended him and not acted appropriately. He could literally talk the entire 50 minutes with little awareness that we were not actually interacting. His need to be heard and to be in control was extreme.

It was not until I met John's wife of 23 years that I

was aware that he had struck her several times as well as demeaned her in the presence of their daughters. He is thin skinned, and the entire family feared his aggression. He was ashamed and greatly affected when she let me know of his transgressions. She told me of these past incidents when she came to therapy without John. In his presence, she feared his anger and listened dutifully to his monologues about her shortcomings.

As time went on I learned more about how John became so angry, particularly with women. His mother, when she was drinking, would taunt him and call him a baby. "You'll never be a man!" On occasion, she called him a "little pussy." His father was no help. He had been beaten up at age nine by a neighborhood boy three years older, and had run home to ask for comfort from his dad. His father took him into the back yard and tried to teach him how to box. Dad's comment: "You have to learn to defend yourself, not run away." Herein lies the root of the aggression.

Resolution and growth for John began when he told me he never meant to hit his wife and call his girls names. We explored what happens in those impulsive moments when he becomes so incredibly offended. Over time, he realized he was defending himself against his mother and father, but in particular he had vowed internally to never let a woman humiliate him again.

Repentance as Savior

Whenever I try to help a person change inappropriate behavior that has hurt others deeply, I try to access the level of repentance they have for the result of their actions. John has a conscience, and he felt awful after his tantrums. He knew he was wrong but could not—at least he thought he could not—prevent his response when he perceived disrespect. As we talked honestly about his awful behavior, he cried and begged me for help. He loved his wife and his daughters, but he knew they could not bare any more of his behavior, and his wife had asked him to leave. He went to live with his older brother and hoped someday he could return and be forgiven. He was deeply motivated to return to his family and worked very hard every week to learn more about his fragile self-esteem and how he consistently misinterpreted a reasonable criticism as a personal affront.

John had difficulties with each female superior in his work as a corporate CPA. He realized over time that he overreacted to female superiors in similar ways that he reacted to his wife. Eventually, he began to give his current female manager more room to critique his work, realizing she was only fulfilling her job requirements and not trying to humiliate him. During this time, I encouraged John to begin exercising regularly to manage his anxiety, and also to learn how to produce calming brain chemicals. He had a difficult time learning how to relax. But John became coachable; he now had a father figure he knew would tell him the truth but never humiliate him. He knew I felt strongly about his abusive behavior, and he accepted judgment when it was fair and not arbitrary. He wanted to learn to be a better man, a respected man, a man who acknowledged the damage he had brought his family and a man who repented authentically. He wanted to be a man who could control his actions, and ultimately he was able to do so.

John is now back with his family, but he is not out of the woods. He continues in therapy, and he continues to discuss situations with which he struggles, and we discuss his thoughts, his reactions and try to place them where they belong, in the past or in the present. John today perceives much more accurately than he did in the past. He is developing empathy so that he can see beyond his impulsive reaction to ascertain the truth. People within his family reacted quickly and with aggression and insults. He is learning to slow down, look beyond the surface and to become a good listener. In the past, he would hear a hint of criticism and be off to the races, but now he has learned that quick reactions are often inaccurate and tend to come from past hurts not current reality.

Me Too Backlash

Candace Bertotti and David Maxfield of *VitalSmarts* conducted a survey of 1,000 online participants to better understand changes in the workplace as a result of the Me Too movement. Sixty-three percent of those responding believed that the Me Too movement was healthy, but 45% of women stated that they have experienced incidents that they have not reported. Almost half of the men surveyed admit that they have behaved in a manner that would today be classified as harassment. Only a small percentage of either gender say that training and policies to prevent harassment and abuse have been introduced in their workplace. The most striking finding is that 65% of men believe it is "less safe" to coach or mentor women.

In her book *The Shield of Silence*, Lauren Stiller Rikleen makes the point that the backlash against the Me Too movement contradicts many studies on gender bias. She cites articles that express concern about a backlash in the legal and financial services industries. Social research would indicate that these concerns are unfounded. In fact, few victims actually report sexual harassment, and her research indicates that the courts traditionally favor the employer not the employee.

Forgive me for possibly being simplistic, but if we act

appropriately and treat others with respect and dignity, then I don't see a problem emerging. Those men who are excessively worried probably should be. The scarcity of training is a major concern; the corporate world will not change without consistent monitoring and teaching. Remember, as was stated earlier, empathic environments do not produce harassment, they produce integrity, high character and a close positive work environment where diversity is honored and all contributors are valued regardless of gender, ethnicity, race or religion.

Hopeful Progress

Robyn is a senior in college who just finished her second summer internship with a national insurance company. She was told that one of the three college senior interns would be offered a position this fall to begin after graduation.

A few weeks ago, she said that she doubted that she would be chosen. I asked what made her think she would not be the candidate. "My manager pinched my rear end as I stood up in my cubicle, and I looked him in the eye and told him that if he ever touched me again, I would break both his hands." Robyn expected that talking to a superior in this manner would end her chances for paid employment.

Later she was asked to meet with the director of the division where she had interned. He offered her a position and told her she was selected because a number of people had heard her response to the inappropriate manager. "We want people who don't tolerate abuse. I want a culture where people are respected regardless of gender, ethnicity or race. Your integrity and your assertive response placed you above the other two candidates." Robyn responded, "I bet you have daughters."

His response: "I have three, all a little older than you, and I hope they will display the same courage that you did in the face of an unfortunate circumstance."

15.

The Truth:
A Soulful Person's Quest

"We must become bigger than we have been: more courageous, greater in spirit, larger in outlook. We must become members of a new race, overcoming petty prejudice, owing our ultimate allegiance not to nations but to our fellow men within the human community."

—Haile Selassie

I AM A GREAT believer in the goodness of human beings. Although I am extremely concerned about the negative societal trends in our world, I do have the conviction that good will prevail. I have emphasized throughout this book and throughout my life that if we expand our capacity for empathy, then we can see beyond the surface and find the commonality that exists between all human beings. Narrow, small-minded thinking, often produced by early conditioning, produces prejudice and hatred. Soulful people, even if they have been exposed to significant prejudice early in life, are committed to being free of irrational bias.

As I wrote in *The Soulful Leader*, "A person who is soulful lives with purpose and a desire to be of service. He or she is not primarily motivated by status or image but has a natural interest in teasing out the potential of a family, community, corporation, community and nation."

Soulful human beings are the voice of reason in the face of conflict; they are not quick reactors but thoughtful contributors. They know how to listen, as they are genuinely interested in understanding not only those like themselves, but also those who on the surface seem different; they are known for finding the common ground.

One of the most rewarding experiences I have in my practice is witnessing individuals shed their old conditioning as they learn to perceive accurately as well as learning to express assertively, tactfully and honestly. As individuals develop these critically important interpersonal skills, they become happier and more interested in serving and giving to others. This potential is unleashed and our empathy is expanded when we display interest beyond our immediate family, community and country.

When test subjects are asked to imagine talking to a stranger on a plane or bus, most people are anxious and want to avoid such a situation. However, when individuals take the chance to reach out to strangers, they consistently report enjoying the interaction and also learning and reducing their fear of others in the process. These experiments indicate that whether one is an introvert or an extrovert, reaching out to strangers is experienced as beneficial.

Expectations of Two Young Men

Not long ago, I was on a plane to Denver for a short layover and then off to Sun City, Idaho to give a talk on Soulful Leadership to a group of executives in the food and hospitality industry. I was seated next to two young men in their late twenties, and ironically, they were both in the hospitality industry. As I sat down

I thought I would continue to work on my speech, but I felt uncomfortable with not introducing myself and making contact with my two companions. They told me of their work in Boston, and how they were going on a ski trip in Denver. After about 20 minutes of learning about their lives, one of them asked what I do for a living. I was in a light mood so I answered, "What answer could I give that would impress you?" They both smiled and began to think. John, sitting right beside me, tall, lanky and articulate, said, "I wish you were a criminal attorney, a judge, a CEO of something or a biotech scientist." His friend Bobby, short, with a middle linebacker physique, and affable, said, "I wish you were an NFL owner, or a MLB owner or some executive in the professional sports world." Well, even though I began this conversation just being light, we really had a great time with their expectations of what would bring them value, respect and joy in the workplace. None of which had much to do with working in the hospitality industry.

So, before I answered their original question about my career, I asked them to be completely honest and tell me if it would make a difference if I held any of those positions and were a Jew, or a Muslim or an atheist. They both answered that it would not bother them at all if I were Jewish, as they each had several Jewish friends. Bobby said he would be uncomfortable with an atheist, because he was brought up in the congregational church and he and his family were always ardent believers. Most striking, though, was John's honesty, "I feel embarrassed, but the moment you said Muslim, I knew I would not want to be around that person. I immediately associated Muslim with terrorism, and I know that's wrong." I asked John where he thought that quick reaction came from. "I don't know; I guess it's from everything I see and hear on social media, TV, and news outlets. I've never really tried to learn anything about Muslims. I come from a small midwestern town, and I have never met a Muslim."

What a world it would be if everyone was as open to examining the facts as John displayed!

I enjoyed my interaction with these two young men; their honesty and openness was encouraging. They were open to learning about themselves and about me. When I finally told them what I do for a living, they both thought they should have known, because my approach toward them suddenly made sense. It was a novel experience which reinforced the point about approaching others, strangers at first and possibly friends in time.

Their wishes for certain careers told a unique story about each of them. I had no doubt that each of them, if exposed to a Muslim or an atheist person in a leadership position, would learn, make adjustments and ultimately grow. They both acknowledged they had no exposure to atheists or Muslims and they knew their uneasiness would likely change if they had the opportunity to know such people.

Our trip to Denver flew by, and I felt that I had just encountered two young men who will not be part of our growing rates of hatred toward difference. I think they are far more likely to be part of an expanding group of young people who value an open mind and an open heart.

Teasing out the Truth

Psychologists describe prejudice as falling into two categories: explicit attitudes that we share with others, and implicit attitudes of which we may not even be aware. Most negative attitudes, like John's uncomfortable feelings regarding Muslims, are towards minority groups. Studies searching out these hidden biases have been revealed in hiring practices, with doctors less likely to recommend treatment for black patients, and police officers more likely to shoot an unarmed black man than a white subject. When these biases are out of a person's awareness, the first step in revealing the truth is to help individuals become aware of their stereotypes. As I have mentioned in earlier sections, this is the work we do in my communication and leadership groups, as well as the work I have cited conducting empathy circles.

People often begin with little awareness of their biases, those that have been learned over many years without being questioned. In an environment where trust is established and openness and empathic listening are highly valued, people are more likely to be open to exploring their fixed views of others. Our discussions have ranged from racial, religious, ethnic and gender bias. Awareness and exposure are key elements in reducing bias. Stranger studies have proven that once we take a chance to relate to someone who may seem quite different, with empathy guiding the way, we not only dispel our anxiety but we rid ourselves of untruths that hamper our ability to relate to a diverse group of people. Studies in the corporate world have proven that companies that employ thinkers from various backgrounds perform better than homogenous groups as they display more creativity, better problem solving and are more able to solve complex problems. Diversity is an advantage, not a hindrance.

So ask yourself what stereotypes you have accumulated over the years. Do you have the courage to share your biases with someone close to you? Particularly the biases that border on prejudice and those that have been used to discriminate against a particular group. John's answer on the plane was encouraging to me. He was embarrassed because he knew his quick reaction was not based on fact but rather what he has heard in the media, from politicians and others who make broad generalizations to serve their ego-driven purpose.

16.

Special Connections:
Interfaith Friendship and Love

"There will be no peace among the nations without peace among the religions."

—Hans King

Two of my favorite books are *Toward a True Kinship of Faiths: How the World's Religions Can Come Together* by His Holiness The Dalai Lama and *Holy Envy: Finding God in the Faith of Others* by Rev. Barbara Brown Taylor. Each theologian details a great appreciation for what religions other than their own contribute to the well-being and spiritual development of their followers.

I am attracted to the age-old wisdom of the Torah and Talmud, as I am of the age-old insights of the Tao Te Ching. I love the Buddhist emphasis on being present, being gracious, appreciative and compassionate, and I admire the dedication to prayer and outreach of my Muslim brothers and sisters. I value the openness of the Sikhs and I am intrigued by the compassion and kindness of atheists, I was taught from an early age that without a belief in God and the hereafter, the human race would be run by greedy, self-interested individuals. Of course, due to my experience with atheist friends,

I know this view is untrue.

At the same time, I disdain the forms of all religions that promote us/them dichotomies and the fixed belief that there is only one way to live, strict adherence to dogma and no room for anyone who disagrees.

Interfaith empathy places emphasis not only on understanding different religious perspectives, but also understanding the people we encounter as unique individuals with identities other than the religion to which they belong. We don't greet those of other faiths as, "Hello Buddhist," or "How are you, Muslim?" **When friendship has been established, when empathy has allowed us to transcend religious beliefs and enter the unique world of another human being, we produce positive brain changes that make us open to diverse opinions and ideas.**

As a result, I have interviewed rabbis, priests, Sikhs, ministers, imams and Buddhists, as well as individuals in mixed race marriages, to gain as much insight as possible regarding racial and religious attitudes that contribute or detract from the benefits of diversity.

Fear and Prejudice

The likelihood that we have grown up believing certain untruths about other religions is high. Many religious leaders and their followers tend to be protective of their beliefs and often fear including other faiths in dialogues that may weaken the beliefs of their followers. As a young psychologist, I volunteered to be our department's representative to the hospital chaplaincy where I worked. I asked a Catholic priest what times services were offered in the local Catholic Church. He was immediately irritated and chided me for using the word 'services' instead of 'mass.' "Are you a Protestant now?" he asked. I was surprised and disappointed at the same time because when he participated in discussions with the hospital rabbi and minister he seemed quite open. As I got to know him better, I realized he was a scholar. He was knowledgeable in all the major religions, and in fact had taught college courses in the religions of man. Usually, when people have exposure to various religions, they become more tolerant and open. I knew my friend had such experiences but in a spontaneous moment I think he feared he was losing ground with his young colleague. **It is not uncommon to think we have rid ourselves of old biases until an unexpected and spontaneous moment lets us know that we have more work to do.**

Muslim Father/Catholic Mother—An Interfaith Family

I recently learned that noted surgeon Mustafa Noury's parents immigrated from Egypt. His father was Muslim, and his half-Sicilian, half-Egyptian mother was Catholic. I asked him if I could tell his story. I was curious how he and his brothers, all born in the United States experienced growing up in a mixed religious family and having names that were not typically American.

Mustafa's father was a surgeon in Egypt but did not practice when he came to the United States. He became a schoolteacher but died of a fatal heart attack when Mustafa was seven years old. Mustafa told me that religion was a mix in his home, hearing about the daily praying of Muslims and also of the various traditions of the Roman Catholics. After his father died, he heard less about the Muslim faith and more about Christianity, although, personally, he did not fully adopt either faith. He told me that he was bullied verbally and occasionally shoved as an elementary school child. His peers would make fun of his first name, not popular until recently when *The Lion King* came along. I asked him how he coped with the taunting. "Luckily, my brothers and I were athletic. By the time I reached high school, I was the star quarterback, and suddenly had status among my classmates. At that point, kids started to leave me alone; the cohesiveness of team mentality made a major difference. My name became much less of an issue; it felt like we were all brothers regardless of ethnic origin."

Once again, we see that when individuals are exposed to those who seem different, and certainly athletic teams allow such exposure, a common ground is discovered and religion and color seem to fade into the background. In addition, Mustafa grew up with a mother who was not angry, not biased and not resentful. Mustafa relates to others with warmth, and a keen interest in listening and understanding what they have to say. Mustafa is yet another example of a young man defeating prejudice and hate through connection and by establishing a bond through common goals.

Mustafa's story reminded me of my Uncle Philip. Philip is an African American, my aunt Donna's second husband. My aunt's first husband did not treat her well, but Philip is a man of great integrity, strong ethics and wonderful character. He is outgoing, and people take to him immediately. By all accounts he is quite attractive, broad shouldered with an athlete's physique.

Philip moved from a diverse neighborhood in Boston to the suburbs with his family at the age of 12. He was one of only three black students throughout his middle and high school experience. I asked him if he had faced any prejudice during those years. He said no. "I was a star football and track athlete, and parents of white kids seemed to like me because of my athletic ability. People would call me out in the street after games. Hey, Woody, great game! And I dated white girls with no problem at all."

Philip told me that his first experience with prejudice came after he finished college and entered the corporate world. He told me of one experience when an HR director called him to her office. "Philip," she said, "we need to take a picture of you for our brochure, because you're the only black person we have." It was at that point, as well as on several other occasions, he realized he was being showcased to make the company *look* diverse. On another occasion, he realized white fellow engineers were altering his written work to make him look incompetent. He actually lost that job as a result. A few years later at another job, a colleague told him he knew certain white engineers were doing this to him but felt that he didn't want to get involved at the time.

I also asked my uncle if he had encountered discrimination toward his mixed race marriage. "It was common in the sixties and seventies, but hardly at all in recent years. It's ironic; my parents taught us to never see color, and I really don't. I make my determinations based on a person's character, and that is why I love your aunt so much."

Athletics in the adolescent years saved both Mustafa and Philip from overt discrimination, and Philip told me that it was the same in the army. "We had many white kids from the South, but after suffering basic training we were united, and color disappeared."

Many marines returning from hazardous duty have told me of similar experiences, at first not wanting to be bunked with those of different races, ethnicities, or those from different parts of the country, but similar to an athletic team, as time passed and mutual experiences were shared, differences faded. One white marine told me that in basic training one night he was putting salve on his blistered feet when he noticed a black man next to him doing the same thing on his bunk. Skin color faded as the pain united them.

A Jew, a Sikh, a Catholic Priest and a Baptist Passover

During the writing of this book, I was scheduled to do a talk and book signing of my previous book, *The Soulful Leader*. I was fortunate enough to meet Sikh Siri Karm, Singh Khalsa and Evan Levine, Vice President of a Boston business. The conversation was interesting as we talked about prejudice, racism, and most importantly authenticity. Siri Karm described his evolution from Judaism to studying yoga with noted Sikh teachers that led him to want to learn more about Sikhism, and ultimately he decided to join his new religion. He talked about the white garments Sikhs wear and how they symbolize being open and inviting to all people. He mentioned how his closest friend is a Nigerian Catholic nun, and he recalled how eyes had opened wide at his attire and hers as they entered a room—she in her Catholic habit and black attire, and he dressed in his solid white garments with a white turban.

Siri Karm has a great wit, and has a wise look, long beard and twinkling eyes when he is about to explain an important point. He has a keen mind and an elaborate understanding of the major religions. As he spoke, I could see Evan's interest peaking. This tall, handsome, 42-year-old man told us of his journey as a leader, initially trying to follow in the footsteps of those who were exclusively motivated by money, ignoring authentic connections, and only pretending to be genuine in order to obtain more production. He noted how these half-hearted efforts to be empathic were easily recognized by co-workers. Evan told us he realized that not being a *soulful leader* had caused him anxiety and despair until he eventually realized that a leader can be authentic and still facilitate business success.

I was curious as to how Evan grew to be so open as he displayed a real interest in others as they spoke and told us how he valued diversity even though he realized that in the corporate world such diversity is often contained in the mission statements of companies but seldom actually realized.

After the book signing, I asked Evan if we could meet, because I was interested in his journey as a Jewish businessman. We met the following Friday and talked for a couple of hours. Evan told me he had never faced discrimination, although he realized anti-Semitism was on the rise in America, and he had experienced racism in his business dealings, especially behind closed doors.

Evan told me that his father was a physician, a man who was giving when it came to caring for others, but had difficulty taking care of himself. He used food to reduce stress, and as a result he developed diabetes and eventually was on kidney dialysis. His father was a practicing Jew, his mother not so much. When his dad was ill, for some unknown reason his mother started attending a Baptist church. The best Evan could discern was that she felt the warmth in that church that comforted her at a tragic time. To his surprise, his father started attending the Baptist church, never giving up his Jewish religious roots. But he also enjoyed the culture of the Baptist church. His father even conducted a Passover dinner at the church, and when he died he wanted his funeral to be in that church.

So now I understood how this young man had come to value diversity while never abandoning his own religious beliefs, just like his dad. It appears that his parents were able to embrace the best of both worlds.

Evan is a man who wants to make a difference; he told me that wants more meaning in his life. "I don't want money to be my God, I want to be able to help others live an authentic life, a life filled with meaning." At that moment, I could envision his dad smiling.

The Learning Continues

The day after I met with Evan, Siri Karm introduced me to his close friend, Fr. Carl Chudy, a Roman Catholic priest. Siri Karm and Carl are both members of the Metrowest Interfaith Dialogue Project.

Carl is a healthy-looking man, tall stature with a smile that is inviting. He relates in a calm, thoughtful manner. His friendship with Siri Karm was evident, as they clearly enjoyed each other's company.

Carl has years of experience as an interfaith activist who advocates interfaith dialogue as an answer to religious hate crimes. I asked Carl where Roman Catholics stand on diversity and openness to different religions and ethnicities, and he told me that Roman Catholics follow the same divide as the rest of the nation, some on the right, some on the left, with polarized political views. He mentioned that there are 70 to 75 million Catholics in the United States, and he has experienced many being open to interfaith dialogue, yet there is a percentage that remains resistant to encountering those of other religions. When I asked why he encounters resistance, he said that it was due to lack of knowledge and an unwillingness to familiarize oneself with other points of view.

Siri Karm noted that western Sikhs tend to be quite liberal in their views, citing again that their white garments symbolize that they are open to all religions. I loved his description of how all religions lead to the same truth-God. Sikhism, he said, teaches him that each religion contains the whole truth, but focuses on a different aspect of the truth.

Islam focuses on humility, Judaism focuses on understanding, and Christianity focuses on unconditional love as evidenced by God's sacrifice of his only son. Sikhism focuses on commitment.

Siri Karm told me that he is sensitive to hate, as he experienced a great deal of anti-Semitism as a young Jewish boy attending Gerard College. That institution was created for white students who did not have a father. Siri Karm's father died when he was two years old, and the suffering during those years, and being called 'Jew boy', led to him having great compassion for all human beings. Siri Karm mentioned that he reconnected with classmates after more than 30 years, and he said, "I found decent men who had been seasoned and were made stronger and kinder by life, men I genuinely liked. One said to me, 'Please remember I was only 16 when I graduated high school. I felt tormented, too, and I never wanted to be like my tormentors. If I did anything to hurt you, I apologize from the bottom of my heart." Siri Karm's classmate had developed compassion and wisdom.

I commented after hearing his story that individuals usually go in one of two directions after being the object of such hatred. Some become haters themselves, while others develop empathy for those who undergo similar suffering. Suffering can surely create empathy, as well as creating hatred. What are the variables that make the difference in terms of which direction we choose? When we have one caring human being consistently in our lives who exudes kindness, love and undying interest in us, it is often enough for most individuals to overcome prejudice and thrive.

I have been privileged in my group sessions to witness angry, even hateful individuals uncover their inherent goodness when they are consistently exposed to individuals who have learned how to relate with empathy, compassion and supportive interest. It doesn't happen quickly, but few individuals can resist the positive responses that have been missing in their lives.

Interfaith Friendship

I have been so impressed with the meetings I have had with interfaith activists. They may adhere to different religions, but form deep friendships based on open dialogue, each embraces authentic efforts to understand each other and promote good from their various perspectives. Father Carl introduced me to long-time interfaith activist Shaheen Akhtar, and I met with this energetic peace advocate the following Saturday after meeting with Father Carl and Siri Karm.

Shaheen immigrated from India with her family in 1976. She has been teaching at local libraries, mosques, churches and interfaith organizations for more than 20 years, building bridges to unite people of all traditions. Shaheen is an educator and the founder of interfaith book clubs, discussion groups, and community forums, and is a fervent believer of the benefits of gathering diverse groups of people to explore the major topics causing our society distress. I asked her, as I have asked other interfaith leaders, if she has faced resistance in her efforts. She said that when it occurs—and of course it has—it is a"clash of ignorance". But she also said that if one person can be influenced to be open minded, then that person's newly enlightened views will spread to others, and so on. She remembered with great fondness a high school senior, Sage Grant, who attended a talk titled, "A Conversation with our Muslim Neighbor." Shaheen gave this talk at a local high school in Massachusetts. Some time later, Sage wrote to Shaheen to tell her that her English teacher had asked the class to write a protest poem about what students think is unjust in the world. Sage thanked Shaheen for the inspiration to write this poignant poem:

The Phobia of Ignorance

Do not fear those who are different
Those of a faith
Misconceived as terrorism

A faith of peace and tolerance
A faith as common as brown eyes
A faith similar to your own
A faith only known for their radicalists

For I fear those who are the same.
Constructing a supremacist society
Roping people further into the hatred
Of individualism
Off of a misunderstanding

I fear those who believe
That there are limitations to freedom
Limitations to the land of the free and equal
Rules of who is allowed a chance

I fear those only capable of seeing the worst
Categorizing one religion with extremists

I fear those who cannot see
Pass the blindness of their misconceptions

I fear those who do not know
The impact of that fear
Longing for the sobriety of society
The dawn of awareness
The day people can walk in the street
Without the fear of being accused
Accused of hating their own country.

Shaheen had influenced this young mind, and I am sure this high school senior went on to influence others.

Be The Change

Shaheen talked of her continued commitment to educate others, bring communities together, and to increase understanding and reduce prejudice. We talked about the increase in hate crimes, and her eyes became passionate when she expressed, "There can be no compromise when it comes to dignity." She said, "We must amplify our prophetic voices, and we must engage in a robust movement toward pluralism; our common future demands this!"

After meeting with Shaheen, I found myself thinking about pluralism: *a condition or system in which two or more states, groups, principles, OR sources of authority coexist.*

My life's work!

17.

What the World Needs Now....

"You may say I'm a Dreamer, but I'm not the only one, I hope someday you'll join us, and the world will be as one."

—John Lennon

JOHN LENNON'S SONG "IMAGINE" is one of hope for a peaceful world. Yet when he was gunned down on December 8th of 1980, his killer, Mark David Chapman, said he was disturbed by Lennon's remark that the Beatles were "*more popular than Jesus*" and by the lyrics of the song "Imagine."

Like millions of others at the time, I was devastated. We were shocked that someone would be so offended by the lyrics of a song that he would commit murder. Yet I woke this morning to my wife in tears as she told me that 29 innocent people were gunned down the day before—20 in El Paso, and nine in Dayton, Ohio. Probably more will die needlessly and senselessly by the time you are holding this book in your hands. The shooter in El Paso reportedly wrote on an extremist web site that he wanted to kill as many Mexicans as he could, blaming immigrants for taking away jobs in the US.

A person's religion, race, or immigration status is not the reason these killings take place. In every case of a mass murder of which I am aware, stereotyping of a particular group exists with little empathy shown, nor any effort given to find out the facts rather than accepting distorted views. When human beings expand their range of empathy, anger and hatred dissipate. In our fast-paced world, we often don't take the time to listen, or to slow down enough to hear what another human being is trying to communicate. If we were committed to developing empathy in our schools, and if we demanded empathy from our politicians, and from leaders within the corporate world and beyond, then our society would experience a shift from exclusion and fear of differences to a deep appreciation for diversity and also diverse ideas. There may not be a guaranteed solution to stop mass shootings, but we must admit that our society is suffering, and that our lack of compassion for each other filters down to those hateful, bigoted human beings who perpetrate hate and violence. Our silence, and our failure to demand more from our family members, friends and countrymen gives the more depraved among us license to brutally attack those that they see as the cause of their unhappiness. All that certain impulsive intolerant individuals need is validation of their hatred toward a particular group in order to feel that they have the right to act destructively with a sense of righteousness.

The United States comprises 5% of the world's population yet we have had 31% of the mass shootings in the world. Mass shootings tripled from 2011 to 2014 in America. Between the years 1983 and 2013, 119 mass shootings took place, 66% were in the US.

The causes of such unbridled violence have been linked to social media, to the desire to be famous, to mental illness, to liberal gun laws, to violent video games and to poor parenting. There has been virtually no mention that we have become a society that values status, appearance and material possessions more than developing integrity and excellent character. We, as a nation, are materially rich, yet spiritually poor. I use the word spiritual to mean emphasis on giving, serving and placing the welfare of others ahead of our own ego needs. As empathy has decreased and narcissism has increased, we have seen a desensitization toward the abuse of others. **The cost of get ahead at all costs is measured in the loss of human life.**

A Society in Crisis

Whoever is a perpetrator of violence, hatred and discrimination is responsible for his own acts. Societal changes, however, do have an effect on those who are fragile, small-minded and looking for validation to act out their sociopathic impulses. As I stated in the introduction of this book, Michigan State University has conducted the largest study on cultural differences in empathy among 63 different countries. **Those countries with higher levels of empathy have higher levels of self-esteem, agreeableness, conscientiousness, well-being, pro-social behavior and collectivism.**

Countries with the highest level of empathy are Ecuador, Saudi Arabia, Peru, Denmark and the United Arab Emirates. The United States was rated seventh. Countries with the lowest total empathy scores were Lithuania, Venezuela, Estonia and Poland. Psychologists who have studied empathy scores for the last five years indicate that there is a growing decrease in empathy among Americans.

In a more recent study it was determined that Rhode Island, Montana, Vermont and Maine were the most empathic states in the US, with the least empathic being Alabama, Delaware, Kentucky and Maryland.

Researchers from Michigan State and Beloit College found that levels of empathy in US states were positively correlated with volunteering, higher well-being, and lower rates of violent crime, robbery and assault.

Two factors are clear: Countries, states, communities and individuals are healthier, happier and less prone to discriminate and harm others when individuals have expanded empathic ranges. What is also clear is that declining empathy is a danger sign for our country. Jamil Zaki, head of the Stanford Social Neuroscience Laboratory and empathy researcher, estimates that "the average person in 2009 was less empathic than 75% of people in 1979."

Empathic Societies Thrive

We can all choose to be more empathic; it is a capacity that can grow and expand with dedication and focus. Empathy training works; it causes positive brain changes that make us happy, generous, and creative. It creates positive connections as it increases trust and a sense of security between people. My personal experience, and the work of empathy researchers, clearly indicates that we can rewire our brains to expand our empathic range. Empathy is expanded through experience and by the culture in which we live.

For most people it is hardest to empathize with strangers, members of another religion or race, or certain groups that have been demonized by select members of our society. **We—you and I—can change the negative trend in our country, and maybe the world, if we don't generalize, don't demonize, and don't make assumptions about people or their choices without knowing the facts.** Empathy, the capacity to understand and respond to the unique experiences of another, is not a quick response; it is a thoughtful response to ascertain the facts about people and about their situations. With empathy we can encounter people of different races, or religions, or countries of origin with a great sense of curiosity rather than with a great sense of fear.

I love talking to people from other countries, to hear about their customs, their traditions and their insights about human nature. Although I was raised Roman Catholic, I don't feel wedded to one religion as I maintain interest and learn from all the major religions. I have enjoyed talking to rabbis, imams, Buddhists and Protestant ministers. I have had to unlearn some of my biases toward atheists, and through discussions I have come to understand how a person can be a non-believer and yet a great humanitarian. Their reliance on goodness in one's lifetime has been impressive to me, not relying on the afterlife for salvation but emphasizing with great intensity how one lives here and now.

I have learned from all these experiences, as they have provided exposure to different points of view than what I had been accustomed to in my life. Once we give up our preoccupation with who is right, then we begin to learn from many different sources, not ruling out anyone or any perspective before we have had the chance to stretch our minds through the expansion of our empathy to uncover new and novel ways of looking at the world.

The Benefits of Diversity

One of my clients recently earned her master's degree from a local Boston college. She, as a white woman, was a minority in her graduating class. Her fellow students were mostly from Mainland China, with a few from India and Pakistan. Marie is an open person, and involved in the Universalist Unitarian Church, still she has always valued the perspectives of others.

"It was so cool to be with so many Chinese students, hearing how life is for them in their society. Most intriguing was how the Indian and Pakistani students became friends here. When they go home they will reencounter the predisposition to be enemies, but I doubt they will accept that notion as they have now seen how similar we all are."

A number of studies have demonstrated that diversity reaps consistent benefits. Juries of whites and blacks spend more time on a case, look at more facts and tend to make better decisions than all-white juries. Diverse ethnic groups cause jurors to question their biases. Multiple studies have found that diverse groups are more effective, more imaginative, and increase profits in the workplace.

Diversity in education has also proven that performance is enhanced when students are with others of various backgrounds, as this dynamic improves creativity, strategic thinking and expands the viewpoints on a variety of subjects. A study from UCLA and the University of Groningen in the Netherlands was comprised of 536 Latino and 395 African American sixth graders from 66 classrooms in 10 urban middle schools that varied in ethnic diversity. Cross-ethnicity friendships increased as the classrooms' ethnic diversity increased. Children who indicated that they had developed friendships with others from different backgrounds said that they felt less lonely, less vulnerable, less picked on by peers, and they also indicated that they felt safer in the school environment. Diverse schools that foster diverse friendships reduce vulnerability.

The excitement that Marie shared with me is akin to my own college experience. My early education was not particularly diverse. My small, blue-collar town consisted of Italian, Jewish, Irish and Portuguese kids. When I left home the world became larger. My exposure with Asian, African American and Hispanic students increased dramatically. I was intrigued as we talked about religion, hometowns, customs, food, and family life. I had never been with such different-looking and different-sounding individuals. I remember thinking that my world-taken-for-granted was so small, and without me even realizing what was happening, my world was becoming larger every day. It is my deepest wish that that process continues all the days of my life.

Conclusion

*"God favors the diversity of many people over the
dominance of any one people."*

—Rev. Barbara Brown Taylor

As I READ BARBARA Brown Taylor's beautiful and inspiring book, *Holy Envy: Finding God in the Faith of Others*, I remember wishing that I could write with such heart and wisdom as she had written. I found myself not only admiring her writing ability, but her dedication to understanding those of different religions. She realized that each had some element of wisdom that her own religion possibly lacked, yet she was able to hold on to the foundation of her beliefs. Rev. Taylor did not believe she had to choose one religion's beliefs to the exclusion of the wisdom of other theological positions.

Every day in our current societal climate we are pressured to make choices. Do you watch Fox News or CNN, do you favor liberal views or conservative? Should you be a Republican or a Democrat? Which side is the right side?

A remarkable study recently published in the *Journal of Experimental Psychology* indicated that those who hold strong beliefs politically display mental rigidity on cognitive tests compared to those who are somewhat attached to a political party. Interestingly, independents displayed significantly more cognitive flexibility than Republicans or Democrats.

Another report by Inter-university Consortium for Political and Social research in 1960 found that 4% of Democrats and 4% of Republicans indicated that they would be disappointed if their child married someone belonging to the opposite political party. In 2018, 45% of Democrats and 35% of Republicans said they would be disappointed if one of their children married someone of the other party, which seems to be further evidence of increasing polarization in our society.

Empathy is the salve that teaches us to reach beyond our own circle and to be at ease with uncertainty. We would be a better people and nation if we focused on taking the time to listen and learn from those who seem to have different perspectives than us. Rather than remaining stuck in our views, empathy allows us to be open to other possibilities. Then we are in a position to make decisions based on facts rather than blindly adhering to our party, our religion or whatever organization with which we identify.

There is a time to be definitive, and there is also a time to say, 'I don't know.' When we slow down, seek consultation with others we respect, and commit to learning the facts, then we are in a position to make determinations. Conclusions about people or issues formed without objectivity are dangerous. As we discussed earlier, pathological certainty is destructive; it is fueled by arrogance and a fear of vulnerability. Yet we cannot, and must not, remain neutral in the face of prejudice and self-righteous discriminatory behavior.

Our society, more than ever, is plagued by racism, Anti-Semitism, Anti-Muslim, and Anti-LGBTQ prejudice and discrimination. We must change direction by employing empathic methods to uncover and alter the rationale that allows individuals to hate and perpetrate sadistic behavior toward minorities. Matching aggression with aggression will not change anything.

Empathy circles, facilitated group participation and deliberate polling focused on expanding empathy has proven to help biased individuals understand how they have distorted perspectives that need adjustment. Exposure to those we fear reduces anxiety and limits stereotypes.

I recently spoke with an Arab American professor of his experience in the United States. His warmth and understanding of what all cultures need to do to thrive was impressive. He reiterated my belief that our culture's competitive preoccupation with status and appearance has sacrificed the development of character and integrity. He talked of the obvious discomfort of his white colleagues when having to discuss prejudice and bias. What surprises him most is that he has never met anyone at a university who admitted, or at least suspected, that he or she might be racist. He commented to me that we all have prejudices; the point of open dialogue is to identify those biases and commit to unveiling the truth. Yet at a place of higher learning, where the human experience is supposed to be examined with courage and fortitude, awareness of one's prejudice or the willingness to acknowledge prejudice was absent.

I have seldom met anyone who was so interesting and concerned about the welfare of all people. His desire to understand, to listen attentively, and his quest for the truth was not only admirable but inspiring.

Does my experience dispel any of your prejudices about Arabs? Be as honest as possible, our world depends on each of us acknowledging our distorted views, not hiding them. I know this is only one example, but I have so many experiences with open-minded Arabs, Jews, African Americans, Latinos, Asians and LBGTQ individuals that I do not think it is an anomaly.

So please join me in what may be the most important

decision of your life—to choose truth over stereotypical distortions. I pray that you will make the effort every day, and that you and I will become part of reversing a dangerous trend in our country, and in our world.

Recommended Reading

Begley, Sharon. *Train Your Mind, Change Your Brain.* Ballantine Books, 2007.

Chodron, Pema. *The Places that Scare You: A Guide to Fearlessness in Difficult Times.* Shambhala, 2005

Chodron, Pema. *When Things Fall Apart: Heart Advice for Difficult Times.* Shambhala Classics. 2000

Chodron, Pema. *Living Beautifully with Uncertainty and Change.* Shambhala Publications. 2012

Ciaramicoli, Arthur. *The Soulful Leader: Success with Authenticity, Integrity and Empathy.* Open Books, 2019

Ciaramicoli, Arthur. *The Stress Solution: Using Empathy and Cognitive Behavioral Therapy to Reduce Anxiety and Develop Resilience.* New World Library, 2016

Ciaramicoli, Arthur. *Performance Addiction: The Dangerous New Syndrome and How to Stop it from Ruining Your Life.* Wiley, 2004

Ciaramicoli, Arthur and Ketcham, Kathy. *The Power of Empathy: A Practical Guide to Creating Intimacy, Self-Understanding and Lasting Love.* Plume, 2000

Cohen, Abraham. *Everyman's Talmud: The Major Teachings of the Rabbinic Sages.* BN Publishing, 2009.

Cox, Harvey. *Common Prayers: Faith, Family and a Christian's Journey Through The Jewish Year.* Houghton Mifflin, 2001

Dawood, N.J. *The Koran.* Penguin Books, 2003

Frankly, Victor. *The Search for Meaning.* Plume, 1969

Hahn, Thich Nan. *Living Buddha, Living Christ.* Riverhead Books, 1995

Hahn, Thich Nan. *This Moment is Full of Wonders.* Shambala, 2015

Kolts, Russell and Chodron, Thubten. *The Open Hearted Life: Transforming Methods for Compassionate Living from a Clinical Psychologist and a Buddhist Nun.* Shambhala Publications. 2015

Kurtz, Ernest and Ketcham, Catherine. *The Spirituality of Imperfection: Storytelling and the Journey to Wholeness.* Bantam, 1992

Le Guin, Ursula K. *Lao Tzu Tao Te Ching; A Book about the Way and the Power of the Way.* Shambhala Publications, 1997

Majid, Anouar. *Islam and America: Building a Future without Prejudice.* Rowman and Littlefield Publishers, 2011

Picciolini, Christian. *Breaking Hate: Confronting the New Culture of Extremism.* Hachette Books, 2020

Picciolini, Christian. *Romantic Violence: Memoirs of an American Skinhead.*Goldmill Group, Chicago.2015

Rohr, Richard. *Falling Upward: A Spirituality for the Two Halves of Life.* Jossey-Bass. 2011

Rohr, Richard. *Breathing Under Water: Spirituality and the Twelve Steps*. St. Anthony Messenger Press. 2011

Rohr, Richard. *Everything Belongs: The Gift of Contemplative Prayer*. The Cross Road Publishing Company.2003

Schweitzer, Frederick. *A History of the Jews: Since the First Century A.D.* Anti-Defamation League, 1972

Szalavitz, Maia and Perry, Bruce. *Born for Love: Why Empathy is Essential and Endangered*. William Morrow, 2010

The Dalai Lama. *Toward A True Kinship of Faiths: How the World's Religions Can Come Together*. Three Rivers Press, 2010

Taylor, Brown Barbara. *An Altar in the World: Geography of Faith*. Harper Collins, 2009

Taylor, Brown Barbara. *Holy Envy: Finding God in the Faith of Others*. Harper Collins, 2019

Willis, Claire B. *Lasting Words: A Guide to Finding Meaning Toward the Close of Life*. Green Writers Press.2013

Willis. Schwamm Jennifer. *A Lifetime of Peace: Essential Writings by and about Thich Nhat Hanh*

About the Author

Arthur P. Ciaramicoli, Ed.D., Ph.D., is a licensed clinical psychologist who has been treating clients for more than 35 years. He is a member of the American Psychological Association and the Massachusetts Psychological Association.

Dr. Ciaramicoli was formerly the Chief Medical Officer of Soundmindz.org and is also in full time private practice. Dr. Ciaramicoli was on the faculty of Harvard Medical School for several years, lecturer for the American Cancer Society, Chief Psychologist at Metrowest Medical Center, and director of the Metrowest Counseling Center and of the Alternative Medicine division of Metrowest Wellness Center in Framingham, Massachusetts.

In addition to treating patients, Dr. Ciaramicoli has lectured at Harvard Health Services, Boston College Counseling Center, Framingham State University, the Space Telescope Science Institute in Baltimore, the Revelry Group as well as being a consultant to several major corporations in the Boston area.

Dr. Ciaramicoli has appeared on CNN, CNNfn, Fox News Boston, Comcast TV, New England Cable News, Good Morning America, The O'Reilly Report, and other shows. He has been a weekly radio guest on Your Healthy Family on Sirius Satellite Radio and Holistic Health Today, and has been interviewed on over 100 radio programs airing on NPR, XM Radio,

Voice America and numerous AM and FM stations.

Dr. Ciaramicoli is the author of *The Soulful Leader: Success with Authenticity, Integrity and Empathy* (Open Books, 2019), *The Stress Solution: Using Empathy and Cognitive Behavioral Therapy to Reduce Anxiety and Develop Resilience* (New World Library, 2016) which was recently published in China. He also wrote *The Curse of the Capable: The Hidden Challenges to a Balanced, Healthy, High Achieving Life* (Morgan James, 2010), *Performance Addiction: The Dangerous New Syndrome and How to Stop It from Ruining Your Life* (Wiley, 2004) and *The Power of Empathy: A Practical Guide to Creating Intimacy, Self-Understanding, and Lasting Love* (Dutton, 2000), which is now published in seven languages. *The Power of Empathy* reached the best seller list in China in 2019 and is to be published in Korea in 2020. His first book, *Treatment of Abuse and Addiction, A Holistic Approach* (Jason Aronson, 1997) was selected as Book of the Month by The Psychotherapy Book News. He is also the coauthor of *Beyond the Influence: Understanding and Defeating Alcoholism* (Bantam, 2000) and founder of The Empathy and Goodness Project on Facebook and Healthy Empathic Achievement on LinkedIn.

He has also authored the Anti-Anxiety App, Anti-Depression App and workbooks *Transforming Anxiety into Joy: A Practical Workbook to Gain Emotional Freedom* (2012) and *Changing Your Inner Voice: A Journey through Depression to Truth and Love* (2012) in collaboration with Soundmindz.org.

Dr. Ciaramicoli lives in a suburb of Boston with his wife of 39 years.

His website is http://www.balanceyoursuccess.com/ You can follow his daily insights at: http://www.linkedin.com/in/drarthurciaramicoli, http://www.twitter.com/docapc, http://www.Facebook.com/drarthurc.

Dr. Ciaramicoli enjoys cycling, spinning, and other sports and his favorite activity is spending time with his wife, daughters, sons-in-law and beautiful grandchildren Ariana and Carmela along the southern coast of Maine.

Appendix

Prejudice Questionnaire

1) Comfortable 2) Uncomfortable

Please read the following questions and answer with number one if you imagine you would feel **Comfortable** with the situation or statement, or number two if you imagine you would feel **Uncomfortable** with the situation or statement. Try to be as honest as you can be. This questionnaire provides you with a general indication of your level of prejudice, it is not definitive.

1. You work with a colleague who declares himself/herself bisexual.

2. You are at a wedding and you see two females kissing passionately.

3. Your brother/sister begins dating a man/woman of a different race.

4. You attend a talk or workshop and realize you are assigned to a group of mixed races.

5. You meet a new employee and are informed he is trans gender.

6. You are asked if you would marry someone of a different race.

7. A complaint is made that a mentally disabled person

is taking too much time in the checkout line at a grocery store and the manager escorts him out of the market.

8. An elderly man working at a local coffee shop had trouble hearing what you were ordering and you later learned he was fired.

9. You visit a relative in a nursing home and you notice that there are a high number of foreigners working in the facility.

10. You meet new people at a social gathering and one-person states she disapproves of inter-racial marriages.

11. Your close friend tells you he/she is gay.

12. You over hear in a group conversation that a person believes contact with other races is likely to produce conflict and tension.

13. In the same conversation someone says that contact with other religious groups produces conflict and disagreements.

14. The person sitting next to you on a plane states that atheists are not very compassionate individuals.

15. One of your colleagues states that black people tend to have low motivation.

16. A friend of yours states that she/he believes they are without any prejudices.

17. A friend states that they believe diverse groups are less functional than homogenous groups.

18. A friend states that spending time with people of different races does not lead to greater comfort with such people in the future.

19. A friend states that the prevalence of racism in our society is greatly exaggerated.

20. This friend also believes sexism is also exaggerated in our society.

Scoring:
0-2 Uncomfortable: Not Prejudiced
3-5 Uncomfortable: Moderately Prejudiced
6-8 Uncomfortable: Quite Prejudiced
9-10 Uncomfortable: Very Prejudiced

Empathy Questionnaire

1. I have been told that I lack empathy by more than one person.

   Yes No

2. I have been told that I am empathic by more than one person.

   Yes No

3. I feel good when I help another person.

   Yes No

4. I don't feel much when I help another person.

   Yes No

5. I feel obligated to do the right thing.

   Yes No

6. I enjoy giving of my time to others.

   Yes No

7. I am uncomfortable when people talk about emotional issues.

   Yes No

8. I am not uncomfortable when people talk about

emotional issues.

(Yes) No

9. I don't know what it means to express empathy.

Yes (No)

10. I understand what it means to express empathy.

(Yes) No

11. I often feel that I miss emotional cues.

Yes (No)

12. I pick up emotional cues easily.

(Yes) No

13. I have been told that I need to be right.

Yes No

14. I don't place much value on the need to be right.

(Yes) No

15. I seldom talk beyond the surface with friends.

Yes No

16. My friends and I have deep conversations.

Yes No

17. I prefer to not be around young children.

Yes No

18. I love being around young children.

(Yes) No

19. I think I tend to take more than I give.

Yes No

20. I think I tend to give more than I take.

    Yes No

21. I find it easier to show animals affection rather than people.

    Yes No

22. I can give affection to animals and people equally.

    Yes No

23. I have often been called stubborn.

    Yes No

24. I am often told that I am easy to get along with.

    Yes No

25. I prefer to talk more than listen.

    Yes No

26. I prefer to listen more than talk.

    Yes No

27. In most of my conversations I talk more than I listen.

    Yes No

28. In most of my conversations I listen more than I talk.

    Yes No

29. I am uncomfortable getting close to people.

    Yes No

30. I feel comfortable being close to people.

    Yes No

Assessment:

Give yourself one point for saying "Yes" to any of the following questions:

#2,3,6,8,10,12,14,16,18,20,22,24,26,28 and 30.

Take away one point for saying "Yes" to any of the following questions:

#1,5,7,9,11,13,15,17,19,21,23,25, and 29.

Total Number:
Very Empathic: 13-15
Mildly Empathic: 10-12
Low Empathy: 0-7

2017 FBI Hate Crime Statistics

(2017 FBI Hate Crime Statistics: https://ucr.fbi.gov/ hate-crime/2017/tables/table-1.xls)

Overview

In 2017, 16,149 law enforcement agencies participated in the Hate Crime Statistics Program. Of these agencies, 2,040 reported 7,175 hate crime incidents involving 8,437 offenses.

There were 7,106 single-bias incidents that involved 8,126 offenses, 8,493 victims, and 6,307 known offenders.

The 69 multiple-bias incidents reported in 2017 involved 311 offenses, 335 victims, and 63 known offenders.

Single-bias incidents

Analysis of the 7,106 single-bias incidents reported in 2017 revealed that:

- 58.1% were motivated by a race/ethnicity/ancestry bias.
- 22.0% were prompted by religious bias.
- 15.9% resulted from sexual-orientation bias.
- 1.7% were motivated by gender-identity bias.
- 1.6% were prompted by disability bias.
- 0.6% (46 incidents) were motivated by gender bias.

Offenses by bias motivation within incidents

Of the 8,126 single-bias hate crime offenses reported in the above incidents:

- 59.5% stemmed from a race/ethnicity/ancestry bias.
- 20.7% were motivated by religious bias.
- 16.0% resulted from sexual-orientation bias.
- 1.6% resulted from bias against disabilities.
- 1.6% stemmed from gender-identity bias.
- 0.7% (53 offenses) were prompted by gender bias.

Race/ethnicity/ancestry bias

In 2017, law enforcement agencies reported that 4,832 single-bias hate crime offenses were motivated by race/ethnicity/ancestry. Of these offenses:

- 48.8% were motivated by anti-black or African American bias.
- 17.5%t stemmed from anti-white bias.
- 10.9% were classified as anti-Hispanic or Latino bias.
- 5.8% were motivated by anti-American Indian or Alaska Native bias.
- 4.4% were a result of bias against groups of individuals consisting of more than one race (anti-multiple races, group).
- 3.1% resulted from anti-Asian bias.
- 2.6% were classified as anti-Arab bias.
- 0.4% (17 offenses) were motivated by bias of anti-Native Hawaiian or Other Pacific Islander.
- 6.5% were the result of an anti-Other Race/Ethnicity/Ancestry bias.

Religious bias

Hate crimes motivated by religious bias accounted for 1,679 offenses reported by law enforcement. A breakdown of the bias motivation of religious-biased offenses showed:

- 58.1% were anti-Jewish.
- 18.7% were anti-Islamic (Muslim).
- 4.5% were anti-Catholic.
- 3.2% were anti-multiple religions, group.
- 2.4% were anti-Protestant.
- 1.8% were anti-Other Christian.
- 1.4% were anti-Sikh.
- 1.4% were anti-Eastern Orthodox (Russian, Greek, Other).
- 0.9% (15 offenses) were anti-Mormon
- 0.9% (15 offenses) were anti-Hindu.
- 0.8% (13 offenses) were anti-Jehovah's Witness.
- 0.5% (9 offenses) was anti-Buddhist.
- 0.5% (8 offenses) were anti-Atheism/Agnosticism/etc.
- 4.9% were anti-other (unspecified) religion.

Sexual-orientation bias

In 2017, law enforcement agencies reported 1,303 hate crime offenses based on sexual-orientation bias. Of these offenses:

- 58.2% were classified as anti-gay (male) bias.
- 24.6% were prompted by an anti-lesbian, gay, bisexual, or transgender (mixed group) bias.
- 12.2% were classified as anti-lesbian bias.
- 2.8% were the result of an anti-heterosexual bias.
- 2.1% were classified as anti-bisexual bias.

Gender-identity bias

(See **2017 FBI Hate Crime Statistics: https://ucr.fbi. gov/hate-crime/2017/tables/table-1.xls**)

Of the single-bias incidents, 131 offenses were a result of gender-identity bias. Of these offenses:

- 118 were anti-transgender.
- 13 were anti-gender non-conforming.

Disability bias

There were 128 reported hate crime offenses committed based on disability bias. Of these:

- 93 offenses were classified as anti-mental disability.
- 35 offenses were reported as anti-physical disability.

Gender bias

There were 53 offenses of gender bias reported in 2017. Of these:

- 28 were anti-female.
- 25 were anti-male.

By offense types

Of the 8,437 reported hate crime offenses in 2017:

- 27.6% were destruction/damage/vandalism.
- 27.1% were intimidation.
- 20.7% were simple assault.
- 11.7% were aggravated assault.
- The remaining offenses included additional crimes against persons, property, and society.

Offenses by crime category

Among the 8,437 hate crime offenses reported:

- 60.3% were crimes against persons.
- 36.9% were crimes against property.
- The remaining offenses were crimes against society.
- Law enforcement reported 5,084 hate crime offenses as crimes against persons. By offense type:
- 44.9% were intimidation.
- 34.3% were simple assault.
- 19.5% were aggravated assault.
- 0.7% consisted of 15 murders and 23 rapes.
- 1 offense was reported as human trafficking, commercial sex acts.
- 0.5% involved the offense category *other*, which is collected only in NIBRS.

Crimes against property

The majority of the 3,115 hate crime offenses that were crimes against property (74.6%) were acts of destruction/damage/vandalism.

- The remaining 25.4% of crimes against property consisted of robbery, burglary, larceny-theft, motor vehicle theft, arson, and other crimes.

Crimes against society

There were 238 offenses defined as crimes against society (e.g., drug or narcotic offenses or prostitution).

By victim type

When considering the 8,437 hate crime offenses and their targeted victims:

- 78.3% were directed at individuals.
- 6.3% were against businesses or financial institutions.
- 3.4% were against government entities.
- 2.8% were against society/public
- 2.1% were against religious organizations.
- The remaining 7.1% were directed at other/unknown/multiple victim types.

Acknowledgements

I HAVE BEEN EXTREMELY fortunate to have the love and support of my wife Karen, our daughters Erica and Alaina, their husbands Michael MacDonald and Michael Chagnon and most importantly our beautiful granddaughters Ariana and Carmela.

I have also been fortunate to have the support of my long-time loyal friends Donna and Philip Wood and their daughter Lisa Westhaver, Gerri and Richard Tessicini, Janice and Jimmy Blackler, Dr's Valerie and Peter Smith, and Dr. Robert Cherney and his wife Mary Ellen.

A special thank you to my longtime friend Mark D'Antonio. Your support and courage to persevere despite being in pain every day of your life has been a motivator for me from the first day I met you. Thank you for the ongoing support and encouragement.

The first person to review this manuscript was my friend Cathy Cunningham. Cathy is one of the kindest, most insightful people I know. Cathy recently earned her Master's degree in Theological Studies from Boston College. She graciously offered to review this book and I am very grateful she did, her expertise in the major religions was most helpful.

I am very appreciative to have such a fine editor and publisher in David Ross of Open Books. I also am thankful to Kelly Huddleston for her excellent editorial and marketing expertise.

My friend Wen Qi, a Chinese Entrepreneur, has been most helpful in bringing my work to his Chinese colleagues.

I thank all the wonderful people who granted me interviews: Evan Levine, Furquaan Syed, Mynuddin Syed, Fr. Carl Chudy, Siri Karm Khalsa, Christian Picciolini, Shaeen Akhtar, Philip Wood, Dr. Frank Caruso, Dr. Carol Cavanaugh, Dr. Eissa Hashemi, Dr. Anouar Majid, and of course all my courageous clients who allow me to enter their world every week.